Lust, Passion & Purpose

THIRTY-ONE DAY DEVOTIONAL TO FIGHT HUMAN TRAFFICKING

**DR. DENARDO RAMOS,
SHARMILA WIJEYAKUMAR
& INDIRA RAMOS**

WestBow Press
A DIVISION OF THOMAS NELSON
& ZONDERVAN

Copyright © 2020 Dr. Denardo Ramos, Sharmila Wijeyakumar & Indira Ramos.

All rights reserved. No part of this book may be used or reproduced by any means, graphic, electronic, or mechanical, including photocopying, recording, taping or by any information storage retrieval system without the written permission of the author except in the case of brief quotations embodied in critical articles and reviews.

This book is a work of non-fiction. Unless otherwise noted, the author and the publisher make no explicit guarantees as to the accuracy of the information contained in this book and in some cases, names of people and places have been altered to protect their privacy.

WestBow Press books may be ordered through booksellers or by contacting:

WestBow Press
A Division of Thomas Nelson & Zondervan
1663 Liberty Drive
Bloomington, IN 47403
www.westbowpress.com
1 (866) 928-1240

Because of the dynamic nature of the Internet, any web addresses or links contained in this book may have changed since publication and may no longer be valid. The views expressed in this work are solely those of the author and do not necessarily reflect the views of the publisher, and the publisher hereby disclaims any responsibility for them.

Any people depicted in stock imagery provided by Getty Images are models, and such images are being used for illustrative purposes only.
Certain stock imagery © Getty Images.

Scriptures taken from the Holy Bible, New International Version®, NIV®. Copyright © 1973, 1978, 1984, 2011 by Biblica, Inc.™ Used by permission of Zondervan. All rights reserved worldwide. www.zondervan.com<http://www.zondervan.com> The "NIV" and "New International Version" are trademarks registered in the United States Patent and Trademark Office by Biblica, Inc.™

ISBN: 978-1-6642-0018-0 (sc)
ISBN: 978-1-6642-0017-3 (hc)
ISBN: 978-1-6642-0019-7 (e)

Library of Congress Control Number: 2020913710

Print information available on the last page.

WestBow Press rev. date: 08/06/2020

FOREWORD

According to a September 2017 report from the International Labor Organization (ILO) and Walk Free Foundation, an estimated 24.9 million victims are ensnared in modern-day slavery.[1] That's nearly twice the number of slaves brought from Africa to the New World over the entire history of the slave trade, before it was abolished in 1866.[2]

It's been a long-held belief of mine, distilled from years of attending the Global Leadership Summit, that "the local church is the hope of the world," and a leadership locus.[3] The church was pivotal in stopping slavery in the past, when Christians initiated and organized an abolitionist movement, and it will be again as we fight a new type of modern-day slavery, better known as human trafficking.[4]

---

[1] Human Rights First. (September 2017). Human Trafficking by the Numbers, p. 1. Retrieved from https://www.humanrightsfirst.org/resource/human-trafficking-numbers

[2] Between 1525 and 1866, in the entire history of the slave trade to the New World, according to the Trans-Atlantic Slave Trade Database, 12.5 million Africans were shipped to the New World. (Only 10.7 million survived the dreaded Middle Passage). Gates, Jr., H. L. How many slaves landed in the U.S.? *The African Americans: Many Rivers to Cross*. PBS. Retrieved from https://www.pbs.org/wnet/african-americans-many-rivers-to-cross/history/how-many-slaves-landed-in-the-us/

[3] Geiger, E. & Peck, K. (2016). *Designed to Lead*. Nashville, TN: B&H Publishing Group.

[4] Coffey, John. (2007). The abolition of the slave trade: Christian conscience and political action. Retrieved from http://www.jubilee-centre.org/the-abolition-of-the-slave-trade-christian-conscience-and-political-action-by-john-coffey/

Through this devotional we hope to provide education about what human trafficking is, how it happens, and provide hope that our faith community can apply biblical truths to combat this epidemic.

Figure 1 shows a typical narrative that results in a child being trafficked:

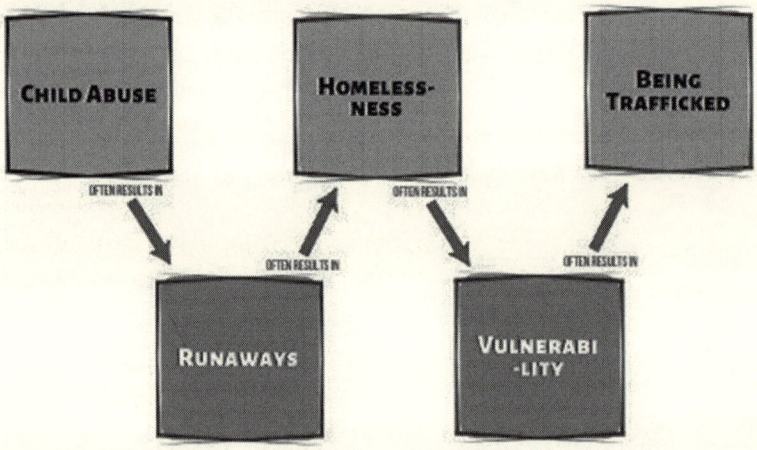

INTRODUCTION

It was in, it was out, it was over. Raped, held prisoner and suicidal, my virginity had gone to a stranger.

I was sixteen years old.

I cried as I walked to the bathroom to clean up, where the shower's pelting water muffled my sobs. I needed a way out; but the more I fought, the less freedom I was given. Compliance had its advantage: survival.

Waking in a cold sweat, as flashbacks of the rape shuddered through me, I couldn't deny the small, still voice that accompanied the memories. It whispered, persistently: *You can help them.*

As disturbing as the remembrances were, it was the voice that terrified me more.

No stranger, the voice had come many times in the still of the night, and each time, I had chosen to ignore it. The more persistent the whisper, the more I wanted to run from its directive. I turned over, praying. I knew that only God could remove the fear, but I also knew that I was evading His calling.

Not now, Lord, I can't. It's too hard! I silently implored.

These little talks with God began to happen more regularly. I would hear Him reassure me: *You can do it. I am here with you.* Not audibly, but in a silent whisper in the quiet of my mind during Bible study. I have always found that it is in private worship and Bible study that I hear God most clearly.

Still, I pleaded, *Ask someone else, I'm not the right person. I'm broken. Afraid. Not good enough.* Over time, I came to realize that God can still use me if I abide in Him and obey His will.

In reading Moses' story, I learned that he, too, felt he was not good enough.

Every woman in the Bible who changed the course of history was abused or neglected in some way.

Noah built the ark during a drought while everyone ridiculed him.

I figured, if Noah was obedient under those circumstances, and God brought rain in His timing, the least I could do was trust Him and see what happened if I took a step forward.

The verses Luke 4:18 and Isaiah 61:1 drew me: "The Spirit of the Lord is on me, because He has anointed me to proclaim good news to the poor. He has sent me to proclaim that captives will be released, that the blind will see, that the oppressed will be set free," (ESV).

To my mind, the trafficking victims are the oppressed whom God has asked me to help set free. "Johns" (the buyers) are the blind, they don't know what they are really purchasing. (We call them Johns because it dehumanizes them). And the traffickers are, *yes*, prisoners—beholden to organized crime syndicates, drugs, and the abuse of their past, themselves trapped in a cycle of violence. They need freedom too.

At the time, I was blessed to be employed by a tech start-up that encouraged us to try new applications with the software we produced. I developed a business intelligence project in my spare time, using predictive analytics to pinpoint trafficking hotspots in the UK, Europe, Africa, and South America. It was an important first step toward my calling, which felt somewhat safer, ensconced as I was behind the keyboard and monitor.

Still, fear filled me. I had yet to learn to trust God or others again. I worked completely behind the scenes, not even telling my husband or family.

Being misused by people in the past had taken its toll. I was wary of people's true intentions, still unable to forgive myself for my past, or anyone who had a hand in the making of those experiences. But, I still sought God's healing.

As a survivor of human trafficking, forgiveness was one of the hardest concepts I battled to accept on my journey to freedom from modern-day slavery. Used and abused by countless men, I will never know most of their names, and many of their faces blur in my memory. A few stand out, and although they only represent symptoms of the problem and are not the cause of the problem itself, it was still hard for me to imagine forgiving them, let alone myself.

I was first trafficked when I was a teenager. Conned into believing I was being hired as a nightclub hostess, I ended up trapped in what turned out to be a high-end brothel.

I've always been a fighter, so resisting this horrible situation came naturally to me—not in the way where you punch people, but in the way where you tap an inner drive to solve problems. And this problem was a devastating, complicated one.

See, traffickers want to break you down—spiritually, physically, and emotionally—so that you rely on them instead of God or yourself for everything. They decide when you eat, use the phone, use the bathroom, sleep, work, or service men.

Coercion is the trafficker's favorite tool. It takes many forms, the most common of which is isolation. Traffickers separate you from family and any social network or support in every area of your life. The isolation may be outright physical or the result of emotional manipulation. The more isolated you are, the lonelier you feel, and the less anyone can coax you down any other path but the one presented by the trafficker.

And if everyone around you is also trafficked—and, mind you, it is part of their "job" to keep you indoctrinated in a system that normalizes slavery—they can contribute to the brainwashing so that you believe this twisted system is the only reality that exists, further isolating you.

Moreover, if all you hear is how pretty you are, and that beauty only makes you vulnerable to abuse, you learn that beauty carries a hefty price. And hearing no positive words except about being "pretty," you come to believe that you deserve the abuse. That you are, otherwise, worthless.

People outside "the life" (as survivors refer to trafficked life) wonder how this downward spiral is possible. However, if you already felt like a disappointment, unworthy, or "less than" *before* you were trafficked, well, after … believing the bad stuff about yourself comes to be so much easier than believing the good stuff.

Repeated trauma leaves its mark on you. You believe you deserve to be hurt, and pain is normal. And people in pain like that only hurt other people.

Forgiving one's trafficker—someone who took every inch of your life and broke you down and molded you into what they wanted for profit—comes with a costly tradeoff. Forgiveness requires letting bitterness go.

Bitterness is the warm, comfy blanket that trafficking victims often wrap themselves in as a defense mechanism against the world. This protective but dangerous cocoon comes with matching blankets of shame and insecurity. The insecurity is caused by an inability to trust. The shame is caused by a belief held by the victim that she is bad and deserved to be trafficked, rather than seeing the experience that befell her as bad, and perhaps her decisions leading to that experience as misguided.

Dropping those defensive blankets took many years of therapy and a deeper understanding of who I am in God. To this day, if I were to step away from God's grace and mercy, it would be easy for me to arm myself with those shields again.

Bitterness caused me to choose poorly and reject genuine opportunities because I didn't trust myself or those around me. Thank God, my Uncle Ranjit, his wife Aru (Aunty), my other Aunt (Periamma) and Grandmother (Ammama), patiently helped me to understand that I was the apple of God's eye. Along with my pastor, the members of our local church helped me see what unconditional love looked like in human form.

I made it hard to love me, at the time. People who can overlook self-destructive behavior and choose to love anyway are pretty special. I dreamt of building a welcoming community like that myself, but still clung to the "safety" of my insecurity blanket.

Enter Rev. Dr. Denardo Ramos, my husband of twenty years as this book goes to print.

A graduate of seminary with a PhD in human services, Denardo understood how to help me heal, while calling me his "Capitamonte," a porcelain doll made in Sri Lanka. (I'm Sri Lankan by ancestry though not born there). He accepted me, warts and all. Starting our family helped me understand God's love for us as His children.

For the first time since I was trafficked, I loved unconditionally and felt loved. When I experienced the loss of a child through miscarriage, triggered by my first tumor, I had the tools to move forward in love and the knowledge that "all things work together for the good of those who love the Lord and are called according to His purpose," (ESV, Romans 8:28).

The voice of God continued propelling me forward, urging me to start a program to save other women trapped in a life of slavery, but I was still unsure that I was capable. I had developed a lucrative career in software, with a niche competency in launching software into new markets. This newfound stability gave me the space and platform from which to take a risk.

Prayer guided me to join a European project to stop child trafficking in thirteen Spanish-speaking countries. I could serve while keeping my day job. I traveled extensively for work, seeing firsthand the lengths people will go to obtain special services from virgins or young boys or girls. I learned how affluence in the wrong hands contributes to the demand for trafficked children. (According to ILO figures, commercial sexual exploitation is big business, accounting for $99 billion of a $150+ billion global human trafficking industry.)[5]

While in Europe in 2006, I read *Rediscovering Church* by Bill Hybels. Hybels describes a community structure that I immediately recognized would aid survivors' recovery. I tucked this idea away, however, and didn't think of it again for years, because I could not dream that such a place existed.

Such community *does* exist in churches around the world. And they are critical in the fight to stop human trafficking.

Denardo and I spent the next six years in Europe, continuing to fight trafficking. Trafficked victims are used for unpaid labor, sex and as drug mules—and sometimes, for all three at once.

We witnessed chilling atrocities, like the insertion of heroin instead of silicone into breast implants to transport the drug. Women often died after the butchery required to remove the heroin, or—if they survived—instead of receiving the money they'd been promised, they were then sold into prostitution, those implants now replaced by silicone. We saw countless girls shoved full and boys forced to swallow packets of drugs, then driven back and forth across borders as drug mules. The United Nations' ILO estimates that human trafficking is the third most profitable crime in the world, after illicit drug and arms trafficking,[6] which often, as we have seen, involves human trafficking victims, as well.

You may think that this only happens overseas, but the U.S. is considered the world's major destination for human trafficking, per a University of Illinois

---

[5] Human Rights First, p. 2.

[6] International Labor Organization (2005). *A global alliance against forced labour*. Global report under the follow-up to the ILO Declaration on Fundamental Principles and Rights at Work, ILO 93rd Session 2005.

study.[7] A University of Pennsylvania study suggested that the average age of entry into prostitution in the U.S. is 12-14 for a girl and 11-13 for a boy.[8] The U.S. government defines any underage prostitution as by its nature coercive, and therefore trafficking. Children of this age don't willingly choose prostitution; it is forced upon them by circumstances or torture.[9]

In 2012, my family and I returned from Europe. We felt God was calling us home, and we wanted our daughter to have an American college experience, ideally at my *alma mater*, Purdue University in Indiana. We moved to Illinois and decided to take a little break from serving while we sought God for next steps.

By accident—or divine design—I drove past Willow Creek Community Church and immediately remembered that *this* was the church with the community model that I had read about all those years ago. Intrigued, we visited and decided it was a great place for our family to hide in the pews. (God had other plans for us.)

In the meantime, I found a job that I love at an enterprise software company based around Christ-centered leadership, with a firm commitment to

---

[7] Hounmenou, Charles. (2015). Human Trafficking in Illinois Fact Sheet. Jane Addams Center for Social Policy and Research, Jane Addams College of Social Work. Chicago, IL: University of Illinois at Chicago. Retrieved from https://socialwork.uic.edu/wp-content/uploads/bsk-pdf-manager/FINAL_-_Human_TraffickinginIllinoisFactSheet-November2015_2_121.pdf

[8] The figure is oft-cited but controversial. Janie Har of Politifact.com states that the original source is a 2001 University of Pennsylvania study. "The number in question is on page 92, under the section 'ages of first intercourse and entry into juvenile prostitution.' The age range of entry for boys 'was somewhat younger than that of the girls, i.e. 11-13 years vs. 12-14 years, respectively.'" Har, Janie. (March 2, 2013). Is the average age of entry into sex trafficking between 12 and 14 years old? *Politifact*. Retrieved from https://www.politifact.com/oregon/statements/2013/mar/02/diane-mckeel/Is-average-age-entry-sex-trafficking-between-12-an/

[9] "The U.S. Government defines human trafficking as: Sex trafficking in which a commercial sex act is induced by force, fraud, or coercion, or in which the person induced to perform such act has not attained 18 years of age." National Institute of Justice. (2019). Human Trafficking. Retrieved from https://www.nij.gov/topics/crime/human-trafficking/pages/welcome.aspx

work-life balance. Even after disclosing my past, the company willingly hired me. Their supportive culture has blessed me ever since.

Our lives took another surprise twist when Denardo and I were appointed as part-time pastoral staff at Willow Creek. Leading 1,500 singles across three services, it was through Section Leader coaching by the Willow team that I gained the courage to finally start telling my story publicly. I discovered that I could mobilize people to fight human trafficking. This newfound impact coupled with my own survivorship of sex trafficking, compelled me to establish a nonprofit organization with my family: Rahab's Daughters.

Rahab's Daughters is a ministry that rescues, rehabilitates, and reintegrates victims of modern-day slavery by guiding them down a path of physical, emotional and spiritual healing.

Make no mistake, slavery is exactly what it is. And we are losing the battle: An estimated 24.9 million human trafficking victims are trapped in a life they did not choose.[10]

Many have told me that fighting a problem of this magnitude is hopeless, and that we can't accomplish such a big change. But I am encouraged by history: William Wilberforce was but a solitary man who rallied for the abolition of slavery in the late 1700s. Wilberforce led the parliamentary campaign against the British slave trade for twenty years until the passage of the Slave Trade Act of 1807.[11]

As Rahab's Daughters and other organizations like it work to raise awareness, I believe that, just as in the past, people will rise up and put greed aside to free slaves and end the demand for them. We have the power to end human trafficking, together.

---

[10] Human Rights First, p. 1.

[11] Wolffe, John; Harrison, B. (May 2006) [online edition; first published September 2004], "Wilberforce, William (1759–1833)", *Oxford Dictionary of National Biography*, Oxford University Press. Retrieved from http://www.oxforddnb.com/view/10.1093/ref:odnb/9780198614128.001.0001/odnb-9780198614128-e-29386;jsessionid=49747F9F4B67B476FF661E23682C08DE

DAY ONE

The Backstory

"Jane Doe" was a young teenager when she was raped by a family member.[12] She was then kicked out of her house. She ended up homeless, alone, scared, and hungry. A "good Samaritan" began buying her food every day. Then clothes, then a manicure. Slowly gaining her trust, he invited her to live with him, promising, "I'll take care of you."

Desperate, abandoned, she turned toward the only person who took care of her. She moved in with the "good Samaritan", and months passed without incident. Until the day she came home to find the refrigerator padlocked. "We have no food and I've run out of money. You're going to have to pay me back for all I've done for you," the "Samaritan" insisted. "One of my friends is coming over. Do whatever he says, and he'll give you money." Terrified to be abandoned again, she acquiesced.

Now, imagine you are a young teenage girl, on the streets. Abuse has driven you from your home. Alone, naive and vulnerable, you have neither work skills nor street smarts. Enter the trafficker, offering hope and seemingly a future, but in the end it's all lies. *You are trafficked*. If you refuse, you are taken by force. This is often the trafficking cycle for teens and minors.

---

[12] For many rescued survivors, their life and freedom remain in danger, so to protect their safety as well as privacy, names and identifying details have been changed.

Devotion Time

Please Read:

Exodus 21:12-16

Let's Pause and Consider:

"Whoever steals a man and sells him, and anyone found in possession of him, shall be put to death" (v. 16, ESV).

- What are your thoughts and feelings on human trafficking, modern-day slavery?
- How do you relate "Jane Doe's" story, and the story of so many vulnerable teens and minors like her, to God's laws?
- Where and how can you take a stand for those affected?

Conversation:

God is clear concerning His laws. It is impossible for me to read the book of Exodus without gaining a good understanding of God's heart. I am bewildered by those who would take possession of a person and deny them the right to live life as a human being.

God has not created us to be abused and mistreated. We are not worthless possessions that can be sold or tossed away as worthless. We are made in the image and likeness of God. We have a value that no man can afford, a price above rubies.

Those who have stolen others, as well as those who partake of the stolen, break the laws of God and of man.

And we, who are captive by the blood of Christ, our hearts stolen by His immense love for us, we have a responsibility to observe our surroundings, to speak out against injustices, and to work to bring those involved to justice. We all have a voice, we all have a say in our governments and communities. Our voices are only silenced when we stop speaking out. Let us open our eyes, ears and hearts to what is happening around us that flies in the face of our Heavenly Father's words.

Let us be aware—because someone's life could depend on our awareness.

Praying God's Word:

Father, grant us courage to speak out against injustices that plague our communities. Give us the words to speak in Your spirit of love and grace. We want to be used not only in our places of worship but also in our communities. Use us for Your glory to bring light in dark places.

Response:

_____

_____

_____

_____

_____

_____

DAY TWO

The Backstory

Are pornography and prostitution related to the human trafficking problem? It's a question we at Rahab's Daughters are often asked. Our answer is always the same: *Yes*. Today, the internet makes it easy to act in anonymity and forget that people on the other side of the screen are also humans who breathe, eat and hurt. Prostitution, in some cases, *is* human trafficking.

Our youngest rescue thus far has been a 22-month-old little girl with a charming, dimpled smile. Her mother was a prostitute; she and a sibling had been fathered by her mom's trafficker.

The girl had been exploited in child pornography. It makes the stomach churn to think of it—and yet, this little girl now has a life of freedom ahead of her, a life where she is free to pursue her dreams, not the abhorrent fantasies of her captors.

Prostitution has been around for as long as humans have inhabited the earth. However, people are not products. In many situations, what leads a person to make the choice to sell their bodies is desperation. (That is, if they even have a choice—and if they are underage, they cannot, and are automatically considered coerced).

Sexual immorality is rampant in our world today and it influences so much of the demand for sex trafficking. If that demand did not exist, a now multi-billion-dollar industry would quickly be rendered unprofitable, and soon, extinct!

Devotion Time

Please Read:

1 Timothy 1:8-11

Let's Pause and Consider:

"…the law is not laid down for the just but for the lawless and disobedient, for the ungodly and sinners, for the unholy and profane … The sexually immoral, men who practice homosexuality, enslavers, liars, perjurers, and whatever else is contrary to sound doctrine" (v. 9-10, ESV).

- What does sound doctrine mean to you?
- What is the connection between sexual immorality and modern-day slavery?
- Why must we as believers live a life of good moral character?

Conversation:

Our aim as believers should be to live a life that is holy and acceptable to God. A blameless life, one that sends a clear message that we are in this world but do not abide by the same moral compass as some others in this world.

Some in the world seem to want to keep others in bondage in order to carry out their own desires. Our laws give acceptance to sin and condone what Scripture clearly calls out as an abomination.

Those who are involved in any action that devalues another acts against God. God loves people. He loves people so much that He gave His only Son for ALL of us. No one of us has the right to take advantage of another.

Let us keep the faith and know that although God sits in heavenly places, He is not far-removed from the evil acts of people in this earthly realm. He rewards those who seek Him and is a just judge of those who do not.

Praying God's Word:

Lord, we want to do what is honorable to You. Help us to keep our eyes on You. Give us the strength to avoid sin but also to call out sin in wicked people. Open our hearts to the pain of those around us and let us be an instrument to set the captives free. All for Your glory.

Response:

_____
_____
_____
_____
_____
_____
_____

DAY THREE

The Backstory

Wouldn't it be amazing if, instead of traffickers, Christians were the ones persuading the most vulnerable among us? What if we could provide options to those at risk that would lead them towards God and away from traffickers?

This is what Rahab's Daughters tries to do. Every year, we organize a mission trip to the Super Bowl city to raise awareness, prevent entrapment, and rescue survivors during the big event. (The Super Bowl, as one of the biggest travel events in the country, leads to an uptick in tourists seeking sex services and therefore traffickers looking to profit.)

Volunteers take part in the outreach in airports, strip clubs, and on the streets, including passing out roses. The roses share our helpline number and bear the message, "*You are treasured.* If you need anything, please call us toll free." Innocuous enough to get past the controlling eye of traffickers, the roses let trafficked women, men and children know that they are seen, that there is help available, and that *they are loved*.

This powerful message sets the wheels of rescue, rehabilitation, and reintegration into motion. At the 2020 Super Bowl, our efforts, in collaboration with other organizations and law enforcement on the ground, led to the arrests of two men, and the rescue of multiple trafficking victims: 105 women and 22 children in total.

We can't end human trafficking alone. We want to equip every church in the world with the knowledge to understand what trafficking is and the tools to help stop demand and prevent entry. We want to inspire and ensure that the Christian community is again committed to ending slavery. It can only happen if we unite.

Devotion Time

Please Read:

Psalm 82:1-8

Let's Pause and Consider:

"Rescue the weak and the needy; deliver them from the hand of the wicked" (v. 4, ESV).

- Why should we as Christians speak up for those who have been wronged?
- Where lies our share in the responsibility for bringing an end to human trafficking?

Conversation:

Our society has become obsessed with greed and lust. We are assailed everyday with schemes for pursuing wealth and messages that more is better. Trust me, my friends, being successful is great and material comfort can be beneficial. However, is it ever okay to put my desire for more ahead of the care and wellbeing of another? There are those in our society who would prey upon the weak and vulnerable to pursue their own gains.

God wants us to sing His praises in the courts, in towns and at our places of business. Asaph did not preach the psalm as most. But, he was clear in his praise towards God. When we speak up for those who have no voice and defend those who have no strength to fight, we are indeed singing praises to God. My friend, our praise is not merely in the words we use, but in our actions toward each other, and especially toward the stranger from whom we stand to reap nothing.

We have a mandate as believers to take a stand and to be steadfast, immovable, and always abounding in what is right for all, not just me and mine. Our voices should rise as a sounding cymbal to declare to a corrupt nation that what they have done to the most vulnerable of people, they did to God.

Praying God's Word:

God, I pray that you will give us the courage to speak up for those who would be silenced by their oppressors. Give us strength to take a stand against injustice and to invoke Your principles into our lives. When we know Your truth we can share it confidently knowing that You are our protector and our shield. Give us the words to say and the heart for all of Your children. Let us share Your hope to those who are hurting. Father, heal them spiritually, emotionally and physically of all of their pains and scars.

Response:

_____

_____

_____

_____

_____

_____

DAY FOUR

The Backstory

As Benjamin Franklin said, "An ounce of prevention is worth a pound of cure." So, let's stand up for our kids, for our neighbors' kids, and for any children we see who may be on the periphery and at risk.

The U.S. Department of Justice (DOJ) funded a study that looked at sex trafficking of minors in the U.S. They reported that the median age of trafficked children is 15 years old.[13] These youth are the mute and destitute whom we need to defend and protect.

Many believe that trafficking only happens overseas, or "not in my town." The reality is, slavery happens everywhere, across every demographic. All children, of every socioeconomic level, are susceptible to being lured into our society's dangerous underbelly. In "Jane Doe's" case, she grew up in a big house and nice neighborhood that belied a turbulent home life. She attended middle school in an affluent suburb of a major metropolitan area. She was the proverbial girl next door.

---

[13] Polaris Project. (January 5, 2016). The Average Age of Entry Myth. Retrieved from: https://polarisproject.org/blog/2016/01/05/average-age-entry-myth

"Jane Doe's" story is not an uncommon one. Risk factors that increase the probability that a child will be sexually exploited include housing instability, previous sexual assault or incest, and parental neglect or abuse.[14]

Stop bullies and build up the self-esteem of our children, so that we can raise up a strong, God-fearing generation who will in turn stop the demand for paid sex with minors. No demand = no supply needed.

Devotion Time

Please Read:

Proverbs 31:1-9

Let's Pause and Consider:

"Open your mouth for the mute, for the rights of all who are destitute. Open your mouth, judge righteously, defend the rights of the poor and needy" (v. 8-9, ESV).

- Why should we, as believers, desire to be used by God?
- Do you believe that your behavior (or lack of action) is an indication of your relationship with Christ?

Conversation:

It is easy for this, our flesh, to become prejudiced and judgmental. Our daily lives and values are impacted directly by those around us as well as the media. Our opinions about what is right and wrong, and what we will

---

[14] Institute of Medicine and National Research Council. (2013). *Confronting Commercial Sexual Exploitation and Sex Trafficking of Minors in the United States.* Washington, DC: The National Academies Press. Retrieved from https://www.nap.edu/read/18358/chapter/6, p. 77.

tolerate, comes from our values—values that were instilled in us, whether right or not, by those in our inner circle, especially in our earliest years.

How we see the world and those in it is based on what we value or perceive as valuable. Our values become a yardstick by which we measure what we see: rejecting people and ideas that go against our personal values; accepting that which feels comfortable; and reinforcing what we believe to be true. By those standards, anyone we perceive as different from ourselves, we may judge harsher than we would ourselves.

God wants us to be righteous in our discernment. To look on others, whose lives are less polished and rose-colored than ours, with mercy and compassion.

We are to speak up for those who are not able to speak up for themselves, and for those who go without. This goes against the grain of a culture that emphasizes who you know and encourages rubbing elbows with the "right people." Christ tells us to speak out about injustice and to step up to the plate to defend the rights of those that society would trample.

When we take such a stand, we inevitably go against the grain. We will likely lose popularity, and this is not easy. Following Christ is about building people and sometimes that means walking a path with few supporters. As Christians, our values are about sharing Christ and doing our part to make sure that those who are different or vulnerable are neither silenced nor ignored.

Praying God's Word:

God, we live in a world that seems to want to bring the most needy of our society to their knees and strip them of any dignity and self-respect. We ask that You use us to stand firm in the faith as we declare that we will be Your instruments, Your voice to uphold what is right. We will not judge and punish people for being born differently than us. Help us to see everyone through Your eyes and be Your vessel to declare that all are precious to You.

Response:

DAY FIVE

The Backstory

Due to the nature of human trafficking, victims have many different needs upon rescue. Traffickers don't often permit the women and girls to see a doctor beyond cursory emergency room visits, where girls and medical staff are closely monitored under the trafficker's watchful and controlling eye. So, most rescues have not received basic medical attention over the course of their time spent in slavery, which could span many years. Survivors also require extensive counseling in order to cope with the traumatic experience that they've endured.

"Jane Doe" was first trafficked as a young teenager; she didn't reach us until she was old enough to drive. Working with ally health care organizations, she received medical care for the first time in years. The examination revealed that parts of her skull had been broken at different times over those years, a sign of repeated beatings for which she was never treated. She also had a common sexually transmitted disease and was diagnosed with a mental health disorder that required medication and therapy.

Part of Rahab's Daughters' mission is to help these women and children heal from the devastating experiences they've had, and to provide support throughout their healing journey. We teach victims that they are not weak; on the contrary, they have the strength to overcome. Build into your community by helping foster respect and self-esteem across all members.

Devotion Time

Please Read:

Ezekiel 34:11-16

Let's Pause and Consider:

"I will seek the lost, and I will bring back the strayed, and I will bind up the injured, and I will strengthen the weak, and the fat and the strong I will destroy. I will feed them in justice" (v. 16, ESV).

- In the restoration of Israel, God says He is the shepherd going for His scattered sheep. Do you feel that each life has a purpose?
- If yes, why? If no, why not?

Conversation:

You know how people come and go in your life and you lose contact with them? As I dove more and more into the trafficking world, I found that sometimes people stop communicating because they have no choice. Their right to decide has been taken away from them. In many cases, they have been excommunicated from family and social circle because of a situation in which they may not have had a say.

I think it's interesting that Christ makes a distinction between the ones who strayed, or just wandered off on their own, and the lost, who no longer know how to find their way back. They have lost their connection with anything familiar. He will seek them both, and bring them home.

I believe that we as Christians have a commission to seek out the lost, just as Christ declared that He will do in Israel's restoration. How do we reach out to those who have lost direction? There is a purpose and a plan for each individual's life. We sometimes do not know the value a life will have in the restoration of the church. But, our goal and our desire should persuade us to move forward in leaving our comfort zones and seek those who need to be brought back to the kingdom of God. We should seek the hurting, the lost, the abused, the sick so that they can be restored and reap the reward of what Christ has done for them.

Praying God's Word:

God help us to value each person. We want to be used to build Your church. We know this means we might have to go looking and searching. Prepare our hearts to receive You and give us guidance. Advise us and give us a clear word to speak, so that each person who crosses our paths will know You love them.

Response:

_____

_____

_____

_____

_____

_____

_____

DAY SIX

The Backstory

It is a truly amazing gift to be able to witness the transformation of a trafficking survivor. Many victims have not had the luxury of a regular meal and, in fact, many had to meet certain quotas enforced by traffickers in order to *earn* a meal.

"Karren Koe" had first been trafficked as a teenager. Over the next couple years, she was twice sold across state borders. Her last trafficker kept her locked in a room, withholding food and sleep, and forced her to serve an impossible quota of men to earn a scant amount of food. "Karren" didn't step foot outside for months. By the time she was referred to us and we were finally able to get her a bus ticket, she was suffering from severe malnutrition, barely weighing in triple digits although she was a tall young woman.

Gaunt and exhausted, with little more than the clothing on her back, she arrived just prior to our annual gala. We got her settled in a safe house (she was still being hunted by her traffickers), then provided her with an outfit to wear to the gala. Overwhelmed as she listened to other survivors share their stories and felt the kindness and support of those in attendance, she wept uncontrollably.

After some time, she returned back to her normal weight, healthy and able to attend school.

I remember having the opportunity to treat one survivor to a nice breakfast at a local restaurant. From the moment I said to her "order whatever you'd like," to the moment the food was served to her, the smile never left her face. Through her smile, I could again see potential being awakened by this small act of kindness.

Devotion Time

Please Read:

Isaiah 58:1-7

Let's Pause and Consider:

"Is not this the fast that I choose: to loose the bonds of wickedness, to undo the straps of the yoke, to let the oppressed go free, and to break every yoke? Is it not to share your bread with the hungry and bring the homeless poor into your house; when you see the naked, to cover him, and not to hide yourself from your own flesh?" (v. 6-7, ESV).

- Why should our fasting be selfless?
- Should we fast for personal gratification?
- Should the afflictions of others be our focus in fasting?

Conversation:

Fasting is a vital part of our growth as believers in Christ. It is the act of putting another priority above ourselves. Fasting allows us to bind the flesh and fully submit to God. That is, when we fast with the right intentions. This scripture shares with us the reasons we should be fasting: our goal in fasting should be to lift up the oppressed, the hungry, and the abused.

Victims of human trafficking are mistreated, abused, oppressed and yet we rarely hear of anyone fasting for them. Isaiah 58 brings us to face the truth about our hearts' intent in fasting.

- Why do we fast?
- For whom do we fast?
- Do we have anything to gain from fasting?

As believers, we must concern ourselves with the plight of others. Fasting is a way to let Heaven know that we need help for our fellow brothers and sisters. It is a direct hotline to the Holy Spirit and should not be taken lightly nor used for our own gratification.

Praying God's Word:

God, we thank you for an opportunity to petition Heaven for those who are in trouble and hurting. We know that You are mindful of them and that You care about them. We ask that You give us for what and for whom to fast. We are eager to stand proxy for those who are captive, poor and oppressed. We want to see Your kingdom come and Your will be done in the lives of others.

Response:

_____

_____

_____

_____

_____

_____

DAY SEVEN

The Backstory

The majority of human trafficking victims come from family backgrounds that are less than ideal. "Jane Doe's" heartbreaking story is a perfect example. When "Jane" went to her family for help, instead of consoling her, getting her help and holding the evil family member accountable for his actions through the legal system, "Jane" was abandoned and left to fend for herself on the streets.

In my own story, I was more the exception than the rule: I grew up in a loving family with my sister and both parents in an upper middle-class neighborhood in New Zealand. I never wanted much for anything. We were reasonably happy. Then, in my teen years, I fell in with the wrong crowd. My parents were having some issues; my dad's job kept him away a lot. Suddenly, my family life started to change. At 16 years old, I ran away from home.

My family's Hindu values focused on book smarts versus street smarts, so, now homeless and parentless, I knew very little of the world. When I was recruited to be a hostess in a high-end nightclub, I naively wondered why so many of the clientele were men but didn't connect the dots. And when, after collecting door charges and serving tea and coffee for three days, management told me I was required "upstairs," I went unquestioningly. I couldn't for the life of me understand why there were so many bedrooms—until I was locked in one. Starved, with no access to a phone, I was given a choice, "if you want to eat, if you want to come out, this is what you have to do." I refused. And then I was raped.

Many trafficking victims have faced abuse, broken homes, substance abuse and homelessness. For some, this means they never had the opportunity to see what a healthy family looks like, or what a functional lifestyle entails.

Throughout the recovery process, and through positive mentorship, victims can witness positive lifestyle habits modeled for them, and develop new, healthy relationships. It is our responsibility to help our communities foster those relationships and positive models, and it's one way we can help end trafficking.

Devotion Time

Please Read:

James 1:19-27

Let's Pause and Consider:

"Religion that is pure and undefiled before God the Father is this: to visit orphans and widows in their affliction, and to keep oneself unstained from the world." (v. 27, ESV).

- Why should we be doers of the word and not just listeners?
- For what reason are we to live out what we preach?

Conversation:

I always find it amusing when I see students attend my lectures and dutifully take notes on what they should know and how they should prepare, then never actually *act*. They are great at listening but not very good at carrying out the tasks.

For us as Christians, church functions like that classroom. We should not go to church and get a good word on how to live a God-inspired life, only to do nothing with that information. What a waste of good information! God has called us to be an example to and for the world. In order for us to lead we must set the example. The best way to train our children to do what is right is to have them see us do what is right. They learn from our actions, not our words.

As Christians, we are to learn Christ's characteristics as shown in Scripture. James tells us that if we are not living what we are being taught from God's word then our religion, our faith, is worthless. We should not be tarnished by the world system of greed and corruption, but rather, we should be saturated with compassion and grace for everyone.

As you go about your mission this week of reaching out to those who are hurting and confused, let's remember to be doers and not just listeners. Let's express God's word and put it into practice with all whom we come into contact.

We should not be deceived by our own actions, rather share God's love with those who most need to know of His love. Let's not be fruitless and faithless. Let's be purposeful in doing what will set the captive free.

Praying God's Word:

Father, I ask that you help us to take instruction with a teachable spirit. Let us want to live out what we have learned through the reading of Your word. Show us where we can better serve You with our living. We want to be people of faith. We want to be people that lead by example. Help us to lead as we follow You.

Response:

DAY EIGHT

The Backstory

Due to the nature of the "work" that many victims are trafficked into, it is all too easy for society to place a negative stereotype on that person. According to the ILO and Walk Free Foundation, many trafficking cases do involve the trafficker exploiting the victim sexually: of the estimated 24.9 million victims who were trapped in modern-day slavery in 2017, 4.8 million (19%) were sexually exploited.[15]

However, what we need to understand is that any person who is involved in prostitution as a minor, *is* a trafficking victim. By virtue of their age, any minor involved in prostitution has been coerced. She or he cannot make the adult choice implied by prostitution. This is, therefore, not prostitution; it is human trafficking. It is systematic, repeated rape, because a child cannot give consent to an adult act.

While the U.S. Department of Justice estimates that the number of children (those under the age of 18) being sexually exploited may be anywhere between 100,000 and 3 million,[16] knowledge of the commercial sexual exploitation of children and the public's response to the problem is still evolving.[17]

---

[15] Human Rights First, p.1.
[16] Friedman, S. (2005). *Who is there to help us: How the system fails sexually exploited girls in the United States.* New York: EPCAT-USA, Inc.
[17] Williams, L.M. & Frederick, M.E. (2009). *Pathways into and out of commercial sexual victimization of children: Understanding and responding to sexually exploited teens.* Lowell, MA: University of Massachusetts Lowell. Page 4.

"Karren" may have been an adult in years when she came to us, but she was forced into this life before she could make an adult choice, as a teenager.

Instead of condemning these people for the things they have experienced in life, we need to extend our hands to help them.

Devotion Time

Please Read:

Matthew 25:34-46

Let's Pause and Consider:

"And the King will answer them, 'Truly, I say to you, as you did it to one of the least of these my brothers, you did it to me'" (v. 40, ESV).

- God is concerned about those who are the outcast of society and plagued with misfortune. Why does He call us to respond to their needs?
- How can I be sure that my actions are coming from a pure heart?

Conversation:

We push and climb and strive for better careers, more pay and a better tomorrow. Believe me, there is nothing wrong with wanting to achieve more and to have a better life for yourself. In wanting to achieve so much more, there seems to be a time when we are so focused on our goals that we overlook the needs of others.

As we respond to the call of achieving more, we sometimes devalue the position others are in, who are less fortunate than us. Oh, it is not an intentional decision. We simply want to move ahead, as quickly as possible, and with very few detours.

Christ tells us to stop and pause. To consider what we have done for the stranger, the prisoner, the hungry and the naked. He cares about those that society can sometimes forget. Those we toss to the side of the road and judge as if they are societal nuisances: the guy holding the sign at the light asking for whatever you can spare; the woman holding up the line at the pharmacy who is not able to pay for her prescriptions because she cannot afford medical insurance; the child who comes to school hungry and is denied free lunch because his or her parents make too much to qualify for it, but too little to actually pay for it.

Christ says that "what we have done for the least of these, we have done to Him." Wow, to truly know in our hearts that how we treat others is a direct reflection of how we treat Him. Let us continue to strive for a better life, not solely to serve ourselves, but to be able to serve others with the resources we have been blessed to obtain.

Praying God's Word:

God, it is our deepest desire to see each person through Your eyes. We want to serve You through serving others. You gave us the best example of a servant's heart. Serving others does not make us a slave or a footstool; it makes us obedient to Your will. We want to serve others as if we are serving You. We want to remain mindful that You are concerned for each person including us and that we are the hands and feet You have chosen to touch the lives of so many different people. Thank You for this awesome chance to show You how much we love You.

Response:

DAY NINE

The Backstory

Unfortunately, our society tends to "blame the victim." All too often, when we share the story of a survivor, we get the question: *Why didn't she just leave?*

Trafficking isn't always enforced by physical imprisonment; victims can be emotionally manipulated and controlled—especially if they are underage— and ultimately brainwashed into believing that compliance means safety, and that they are worthless.

If we wish to see change in the world, we need to be the change. When we meet someone, we must meet them where they are with empathy. Every day, we make difficult decisions and trafficking victims aren't any different. A trafficking victim's decisions are based on survival; they must make the decision to either submit to their trafficker's demands or perish. We must be vigilant, more attentive than the trafficker to the populations most at risk.

What gets me is, after "Jane Doe" moved in with her trafficker, before he turned her out, *he enrolled her in school*. (It was a way he continued winning her trust; things seemed "normal.") I can't help but wonder:*Were there no red flags?* Teachers, social workers, peers, interacted with "Jane Doe" every day. In our educational programs, we teach education and health staff how to detect when a person may be trafficked. To look beyond our own prejudice and bias to see: *Is this person in danger? Do they need my help?*

Devotion Time

Please Read:

Zechariah 7:8-14

Let's Pause and Consider:

"Do not oppress the widow, the fatherless, the sojourner, or the poor, let none of you devise evil against another in your heart" (v. 10, ESV).

- Do we really look after the widows and those without parents in our communities and churches?
- There are many scriptures that give clear instructions around widows and orphans. Why do you think this is important to God?

Conversation:

Zechariah had a word from God for the people of his day. It warned of punishment for rejecting God's demands. The people were given clear instructions from the heart of God on how to treat orphans and widows and foreigners. God also demanded that they not have evil and malice in their hearts towards others. But the people refused to listen and began to ignore God's orders.

How easy is it to assume a worldview where one sees those less fortunate than us as inferior? The world sees orphans and widows and foreigners and the poor as rejects who "bleed the system" and "bring down our communities." The people in these groups are not like "us" so they should not be treated the same nor have the same privileges. This is not the will of God and is not in accordance with His demands.

It can also be easy for some in the world to use the vulnerability of the less fortunate for personal gain, to take advantage of someone's pitfalls in order to benefit their evil desires. Let us be clear that God wants us to love and show compassion to those who are not in our "league." If we expect God to hear us when we call, then we must not turn a deaf ear to His words.

Praying God's Word:

God, we ask that You help us to be more like You. We never want to be disobedient to You. We want to be open for You to use us. Touch our hearts so that we do not fall prey to the world's corrupt system. We always want to be obedient to Your words and how You want us to care for others. Help us to keep a pure heart toward those unlike ourselves and our inner circle. Help us to trust that You want us to be a blessing to our friend and the foreigner just the same.

Response:

_____

_____

_____

_____

_____

_____

_____

DAY TEN

The Backstory

Human trafficking is modern-day slavery. Through rescue and rehabilitation, we at Rahab's Daughters teach these former victims that they are capable of living a life that is free. Free from servitude, debt bondage, and dysfunctional lifestyles. Through this freedom, victims grow into survivors.

The road to rehabilitation and reintegration is not a straight one. There is a high recidivism rate among trafficking survivors.

As I explained in an interview on *Voices in the Wilderness* Christian TV, "Once I got out, I had a little bit of money, and [even though] I ran away as far as I could get, I was a high school dropout. I didn't have any skills. *At that point I didn't think I could do anything else.*"

That's why Rahab's Daughters offers a "cradle-to-grave" solution. Unlike other programs that limit how often a survivor can return or refuse to take her back within ninety days of leaving, Rahab's Daughters believes in unconditional love. We're here for them, no matter what. We will always forgive whatever craziness occurred and help the survivor. We always provide extra grace, for these who need it more than most. Based on Christian principles, we forgive first and ask questions later.

Devotion Time

Please Read:

Romans 8:12-17

Let's Pause and Consider:

"For you did not receive the spirit of slavery to fall back into fear, but you have received the Spirit of adoption as sons, by whom we cry, 'Abba! Father!'" (v. 15, ESV).

- Freedom means different things to different people. What does your freedom in Christ mean to you?
- How does your freedom in Christ set you free from the bondage of sin?

Conversation:

I am so thankful for my freedom as a citizen of this country. When I turn on the news and see what is happening to Christians around the world, I celebrate the blessing of being born in the United States. That said, one cannot ignore the headlines of racial hostility and the rampant demise of those who are poor and unable to fight for their right to be heard. This country that I love seems to be heading in a direction that desires to oppress those who cannot stand up for themselves. The liberties that I so treasure seem to be on a chopping board, awaiting execution.

But I hold firm to the fact that my freedom in this world does not rely solely on my country of birth but rather on a God who rebirthed me. I am a new creation with a liberty in a different kingdom. I have been set free not by the laws that make this nation great, but rather by the redeeming power of the Holy Spirit that lives inside of me.

There are so many people who rely only on the freedoms afforded by man and never partake in the ultimate freedom, freedom from sin. The Bible tells us that we have been made free though Christ. We are no longer indebted to sin but liberated through the spirit.

Christ's liberty is for everyone who accepts Him and makes a conscious choice to follow him. We, as believers, must share this good news with those who live in bondage each day, that Christ has come to make them free. No more do they have to fret about this fleshly kingdom's freedoms being threatened, because Christ has given us freedom. Freedom from sin and shame which can never be taken away.

Praying God's Word:

God, when I think of what You went through on the cross to secure my salvation and freedom, my heart leaps with joy and admiration. I am so thankful and grateful to You for loving me so much that You declared my freedom through the cross. Help me to be free to others with my resources, my time, and my life. I understand that to sacrifice looks different for each person. Help me to know that sacrifice has the greatest meaning when it is my greatest sacrifice.

Response:

_____

_____

_____

_____

_____

_____

DAY ELEVEN

The Backstory

Roughly only 1 in 100 trafficking victims will ever be rescued, according to a senior UN official.[18] This statistic reflects a number of factors.

For one, the sheer enormity of the trafficking problem and the limited resources of the nonprofits, governmental agencies and other organizations trying to make a difference.

There are so many hurdles that each rescue must overcome, from getting away from her captors safely, getting healthy and clean, to staying out of the traffickers' grasp and on a path to contribute as a free citizen—each with its complexities, hiccups and potential failure.

Case in point: transportation. Transportation is always the first major hurdle. People think that government organizations and law enforcement cover those expenses, but they don't even have budget to cover a fast food meal for the victim on her journey. (Organizations like Rahab's Daughters and the National Runaway Hotline take care of that.)[19]

---

[18] UN News. (29 July 2016). "Only one out of 100 people are rescued" from human trafficking. Retrieved from https://news.un.org/en/audio/2016/07/615462

[19] The National Runaway Safeline will help cover the cost of bus tickets, if the trafficked victim is old enough to travel by herself (ages 12 to 21), through the Home Free program. Otherwise, we must find other means. National Runaway Safeline. (2019). Retrieved from https://www.1800runaway.org/2008/07/getting-home-free/

Although it would be preferable to put the survivor on a plane or train, both require ID—of which most victims have been stripped by their traffickers—along with property, choices, and dignity. They can get across the country on a bus without ID, but it's not ideal. It's a long ride, people are preying on them the whole time, and the victims are scared out of their minds. Sometimes, however; as it was in "Karren's" case, where she had little more than the clothes on her back— let alone a photo ID— it's our only option.

Most importantly, and above all, the trafficking victim has to want and be willing to be rescued; to leave the misery that has become her comfort zone because the familiar is less scary than the unfamiliar world of life outside "the life." She has to deem herself worthy of rescue.

Devotion Time

Please Read:

Psalm 46:1- 11

Let's Pause and Consider:

"God is our refuge and strength, a very present help in trouble" (v.1, ESV).

It is unmistakable that many of us create our own prisons. We chain ourselves to our own self-doubt and fear. Everyone has their own unique chains, holding them in place and preventing them from moving forward.

- Ask yourself, what chains have I built around myself?

Conversation:

For so many of us, it is our fear of the unknown that causes us to remain stagnant. We, too, become slaves to our own fears by never venturing outside our comfort zones. We often find ourselves in uncomfortable positions that require us to make difficult decisions. We view the situation in front of us as if we're looking at it through a microscope, blind to the larger picture or the world around us. We may know what we need to do to improve our situation, but remain paralyzed by the overwhelming desire to remain comfortable.

This is the time when we are required to call upon what we have learned of God. This is when we need to call upon Him and rely on the strength with which He has gifted us. Our faith in God will carry us through. We must make this effort to break the chains we have created and free ourselves from our self-made prisons.

Praying God's Word:

God, help me to see You and not my situation. I want to know You in a way that even my doubts cannot affect the outcome. I pray that all that is within me will shout YES in the midst of my mind saying no. Help me to know that You are working on my behalf and that I am not alone in any situation no matter how immovable that situation may seem.

Response:

_____

_____

_____

_____

_____

_____

DAY TWELVE

The Backstory

Feelings of hopelessness are an all too common symptom of being exposed to multiple traumatic events. Through extensive rehabilitation, survivors are able to regain their strength, and along with that strength, a renewed sense of hope for life.

"Yvonne Yoe" was pregnant when we found her as a teenager. Her trafficker, also the baby's father, wouldn't allow her prenatal care. Her friend, "Paula", had been rescued by us before referring "Yvonne" to us. "Paula" came with a three-day-old baby in tow, also fathered by the same trafficker. He had forbidden her baby formula until she brought in a minimum amount of money, pushing her to the breaking point. (Traffickers often use their victim's children, a natural result of systematic, daily rape by them and the Johns, to further manipulate and control them).

After a year and successful participation in our Moms and Babies program, both girls and babies are healthy and safe. In gratitude, "Yvonne" named her baby Rose, for the rose she received from Rahab's Daughters. A rose that changed her life.

Devotion Time

Please read:

Psalm 39: 7-8

Let's pause and consider:

"And now, O Lord, for what do I wait? My hope is in You" (v.7, ESV).

- There are even those in the faith who lack hope. When things get hard where do you go for hope?

Conversation:

Imagine being beaten and threatened daily. Imagine being denied food and sleep, or formula for your newborn infant, until a certain amount of money is made, while being given only one means of making that money. Imagine being so mistreated that all hope for living is fading away, that you are close to giving up on yourself, that choosing death over life seems preferable. There is no alternative, nowhere to go, and no one to turn to.

Although we do not all experience this level of maltreatment, we all face situations that cause us to want to give up hope. It may be that we feel we should give up hope for the salvation of a loved one, for the healing of an aging parent or for the addictions of a child.

Even the most spirited among us sometimes need a reminder of where our hope comes from and in whom our hope is placed.

Praying God's Word:

God, as we face different challenges and situations in our lives, we know that we are not alone. We ask that You remind us that our hope is in You. That we can turn to you no matter what. We find peace in knowing that we can rely on you to be with us and to bring us out on the other side of whatever difficulty we face.

Response:

DAY THIRTEEN

The Backstory

Recovery from human trafficking is not a straight line. The road to recovery is filled with ups and downs. It is common for a survivor to return to their trafficker multiple times before finally accepting the help that they need to escape.

Within a few months of being in the group home, "Jane Doe" ran away. Then she returned of her own accord, then ran away again. This pattern repeated several times over before "Jane" committed to staying. Along the way she got hooked on drugs and dated some unsavory boyfriends—one of whom was really a trafficker, charging extra if she had unprotected sex. "Jane" ended up pregnant, not knowing who fathered the baby.

For most trafficking survivors, the path to normalcy is a complicated one. They often come and go quite a bit, with a high percentage returning to "the life," a familiar one for which they understand the rules and expectations, as grim as they may be—as opposed to choosing the safe, healthy, and terrifyingly *unfamiliar* life outside their trafficker's grasp.

Now, "Jane" is sober, her baby is beautiful, and she's started over. She still has a long way to go, but she's out, she's safe, she has three meals a day, she has a roof over her head, and she has medical care. For the first time in four long, violent years, she is surrounded by people who have faith in her.

Devotion Time

Please read:

Romans 5:1-2

Let's Pause and consider:

"Therefore, having been justified by faith, we have peace with God through our Lord Jesus Christ. Through whom we have also obtained access by faith into this grace in which we stand, and we rejoice in hope of the glory of God" (v.1-2, ESV).

Faith is easy to have when life is perfect and everything is going according to plan. Then, there is nothing out of sync with our faith.

- What do we believe in when nothing is going according to our plans?
- What do we believe when our efforts have not produced our desired outcomes?

Conversation:

Faith is what we have when we believe in something, even though we can't see or prove it. Faith is what we have in our belief that God is God, and that He loved us so much that He gave His only Son for our redemption.

There are hundreds of thousands of young girls and boys who are being held as slaves of human trafficking. They did not choose this lifestyle. They have hopes and dreams. Before they were trafficked, they had faith that one day they would grow up and have a family, a job, buy a car or even just have the chance to go to prom, like any other child.

This story can change quickly when you are forcibly taken from everything you know and those you love. How can you believe, and in whom do you have faith when nothing is working out? You can't escape. You're trapped.

It is sometimes in our darkest hours and most horrific situations that Christ will touch our hearts and we will begin to believe. We will believe even though our situation shows no signs of changing. We will begin to have faith that things will get better. That some way and somehow we will get through. That no matter the circumstances, we are going to make it through.

Praying God's Word:

In our darkest hour, You are there. When we can't see your way, You are still leading us. When everything seems to be going wrong, You are here with us. Jesus, thank You for increasing our faith. Sometimes nothing seems to have changed, but we know that You are in control. We have faith that You are working everything according to Your plan for our lives. We may not understand Your plan or why we have to go through such pain for the manifestation of Your plan. Still, we have chosen to trust You. Thank You for increasing our faith.

Response:

_____

_____

_____

_____

_____

_____

DAY FOURTEEN

The Backstory

In the early stages of trafficking, victims are often "groomed" by their traffickers. The traffickers may pose as a close and concerned friend, or even initiate an intimate relationship with the victim. The victim may even fall in love with their trafficker.

This was exactly "Jane Doe's" story. Her trafficker began as a "good Samaritan," purchasing food for her every day at the nearby fast food restaurant. Then he became a father figure of sorts, providing clothing and getting her nails done. Had she known what to watch for, this may have struck her as suspicious.

With 20/20 hindsight, we see that her trafficker was grooming "Jane" before she could know what was happening. After she moved in with him, he changed from father figure to "boyfriend." As a minor in a relationship with a man many years her senior, the law would regard this as statutory rape.

However, from the perspective of a child who hasn't experienced what healthy love from a parent looks like, it can be hard to tell the difference. Especially when you are desperately clinging to someone who seems to be your only hope and love.

At this point the trafficker had earned the trust and molded the victim to the desired role. That is the moment at which the padlock appears on the refrigerator or the room gets locked, and the victim is forced against her will to join this industry. This is when the victim begins being trafficked.

Devotion Time

Please Read:

Leviticus 19:17-18

Let's Pause and Consider:

"You shall not take vengeance or bear a grudge against the sons of your own people, but you shall love your neighbor as yourself: I am the Lord," (v.18, ESV).

- Is there a person in your life that you feel has wronged you?
- What would it feel like to let go of the weight of the grudge you are holding?

Conversation:

It can be extremely difficult at times to turn the other cheek. It is even more difficult to sincerely have a receptive heart toward those who have legitimately wronged us. To have a piece of jewelry stolen from us would be a terrible thing. But for those who had their innocence stripped from them day and night by complete strangers … These victims were beaten and raped many times. Tortured, by any other name.

How can you love your abuser? I assure you, my friend, that it is no easy feat. It is hard for me to turn the other cheek if someone cuts me off on the road, let alone love the very person or persons that have taken life itself from my spirit. The act takes unspeakable strength.

However, my friends, I can testify that it is possible through the love of God. Even in the times that we feel unloved, He loves us and waits for us to turn and run to Him. It is not always easy to do, but by opening our hearts towards God and allowing ourselves to receive His love, it is very possible. God's love is so strong that as we allow Him to saturate our very being, we find the strength to love even the most horrific oppressors and abusers.

Praying God's Word:

God, show us how to love. We have been in a place of hate towards our enemies, those who have wronged us in so many ways, for so long. Help us to accept what You have so freely given to us: Your love. I pray that as Your love overtakes us, it will overflow and we will be able to look past the faults and wrongs of others and see them through Your eyes. We will develop agape love for our enemies, as well as for our neighbors.

Response:

_____

_____

_____

_____

_____

_____

DAY FIFTEEN

The Backstory

Shaming victims is a tactic commonly used by traffickers in order to maintain control. As Rachel Lloyd writes in her memoir, *Girls Like Us: Fighting for a World Where Girls Are Not for Sale*, "Like any subculture, American [trafficking] culture has its own terminology and slang, all of which is about humiliation and degradation ... Four hundred years after slavery, traffickers are using the same lines, the same rationale, the same tactics as their predecessors in the antebellum South."[20]

The repeated messages begin to shape the minds of the victims until they actually begin to believe the lies they are told.

Devotion Time

Please Read:

Ephesians 1:3-10

Let's Pause and Consider:

"In Him we have redemption through His blood, the forgiveness of our trespasses, according to the riches of His grace" (v.7, ESV).

---

[20] Lloyd, Rachel. (2011). *Girls Like Us: Fighting for a World Where Girls are Not for Sale.* New York: HarperCollins Publishers. P. 95-97.

- Many of us have experienced feelings of shame or guilt for things we've done. Who did you turn to in order to let go of these feelings?
- Are you still holding onto feelings of shame and guilt, are they weighing you down?
- Picture your life, freed from the shame. How does a life of freedom look?

Conversation:

Wow, to experience the redeeming power of God is remarkable. To know that none of our wrong deeds are held against us is mind blowing. We know that Christ gave the ultimate sacrifice, His life, for the forgiveness of our sins. We are now justified and redeemed. We have a fresh start each and every day.

Most of us know just how much Christ gave to show His love towards us. We get to live it every day in our homes, jobs, and just day to day lives. However, there are those who are led to believe that they can never be forgiven for their wrongs and that nothing they do will ever be good enough for them to be made right.

This is just another way that victims of human trafficking are controlled. They are led to believe that not only what they are doing is their fault, but that no one will ever see past the things they have done. The stigma will haunt them for the rest of their lives. No one will accept them.

This is a tactic used by traffickers to keep their victims weighed down with guilt, humiliation, and fear. Fear in believing that where they are is the best place for them because, after all, at least they are accepted just as they are. They are with others just like them.

My friends, we know that this is not how the story was written. There is forgiveness for each of us no matter what we have done or what situation we find ourselves in. God's grace is sufficient for each of us because in Christ we all are just like the other. We have been forgiven.

Praying God's Word:

Father, thank You for Your sacrifice in order that we may enjoy Your forgiveness. We pray for our sisters and brothers who are held in fear by the grips of sin. We ask that You let them experience what it feels like to be redeemed. And that Your redeeming power knows no limits and has no borders. Let our brothers and sisters who fear that they will not be accepted, know that in You we are all bought with a price and we are all partakers of Your forgiveness.

Response:

_____

_____

_____

_____

_____

_____

_____

DAY SIXTEEN

The Backstory

In many cases, it is very difficult for a trafficking survivor to accept the help of a rescuer. Their trust is broken and battered, so rescuers become viewed with suspicion. Survivors will "push the buttons" of rescuers in order to test their limits, and see whether the rescuer will turn to the same cruelty to which they've become accustomed.

To counteract this tendency, we always put someone who has physically gone through this experience—a fellow trafficking survivor—on the rescue team because we want the victim to immediately relate to someone. Survivors don't believe anyone else could possibly understand what they've gone through. It's very hard for them to explain their experience and open up. We start there.

We also have two German Shepherds on our team. The canines serve as guard dogs, protectors, and once the rescue is in the car and being transported, therapy dogs of a sort. A dog immediately puts the survivor at ease, even as her guard remains up with the humans in the vehicle.

It is hard for survivors to accept grace from the rescue teams – and yet, it is exactly that grace that we must cultivate so that we can continue to love, be patient and compassionate, even as we are tested, and our buttons pushed. Cultivating grace in your community is a way to ease survivors› transition back into society.

Devotion time

Please Read:

2 Corinthians 12:9-10

Let's Pause and Consider:

"And He said to me, 'My grace is sufficient for you, for my power is made perfect in weakness'" (v.9, ESV).

It is often difficult to be vulnerable enough to admit our weaknesses or shortcomings to others—or in the case of the survivors, to trust others once their trust has been so devastatingly broken.

- Weaknesses, however, are what make us human. We tend to focus much of our time and energy on improving our weaknesses. What would life be like if we dedicated that much energy instead on increasing our strengths?
- What are your strengths?

Conversation:

It is satisfying to know that God's grace is sufficient for us. It's really simple; it is all we need. No matter where we are in our lives, His grace is more than enough. When a trafficker forces a victim into situations that no human being should have to endure, it is in complete opposition to the grace of God.

Grace will never cause us harm nor force us into a life that is harmful to ourselves or to others. Victims can find grace difficult to receive, especially since they have experienced so little. Most times they are in the harshest of situations and held under threat of even harsher penalties. Even a "good" day is one characterized by hate and violence.

We who have been flooded by God's grace can sometimes take it for granted. We just know it's there and we don't really think anymore of it. Yet for so many, grace is not an everyday gift given by the hands of their oppressors. Even in the midst of their worst situations, God has more than enough grace for each and every one of us. We can reap the benefits of God's grace in the middle of our problems and circumstances, and share this grace with those around us. His grace is all we need to surround us. We are all sinners saved by God's grace.

Praying God's Word:

God, I thank You for my sisters and brothers who have experienced Your grace as I have experienced it. Most of all, I thank You for Your overflow on my sisters and brothers who aren't so sure of Your grace. Grace is not something I believe to be readily available to them. I ask that You make them know that they, too, are a recipient of Your grace. That even at their weakest point, You will show Your strength and power and pour out grace for them.

Response:

_____

_____

_____

_____

_____

_____

_____

DAY SEVENTEEN

The Backstory

A simple act of defiance, such as saying "NO" to a trafficker can unfortunately be punishable by severe beatings and even death. When I was imprisoned at the nightclub, I could hear the screaming coming from the other rooms.

The founder of GEMS, Girls Education and Mentoring Services, shares the story of a trafficker who regularly beat one of the girls she helped until she was unconscious. When the girl learned that another young woman who had come into the GEMS office some years later "belonged" to him, she warned, "He can be a pretty violent guy, sweetie," (an understatement).

The girl, whom the trafficker had trafficked when she was young, replied that she knew. She relayed a winding and complicated story that ended with another girl being dragged out of the house naked and run over several times with his moving SUV. What had triggered the harsh punishment? The girl had been "talking back."[21]

The sad truth of the matter is that, even with as many success stories as Rahab's Daughters has, not all our attempted rescues will make it.

---

[21] Lloyd, p. 58.

Devotion Time

Please Read:

Ephesians 2:1-7

Let's Pause and Consider:

"But God, being rich in mercy, because of the great love with which He loved us" (v.4, ESV).

Children are what come to my mind when I think of discipline or disobedience. When we are very young, we don't yet know or understand the differences between right and wrong until these expectations are taught to us. It is amazing to think that God takes us as His children, and teaches us right and wrong, no matter our age.

Conversation:

What a joy it is to know that we have a just judge. He is a judge who is more concerned with perfecting us than with punishing us. I don't know about you, but I find so much peace in knowing that my sinful nature will not stand in the way of mercy. There is nothing any of us can do that will extend beyond mercy's reach.

We are all sinners who deserve penalties for our wrongs. Romans 5:8 is clear that "while we were yet sinners, Christ died for us." He died to extend the most massive, explosive amounts of mercy to make us perfect in His sight.

My friends, let us not forget the teenaged girls and boys who are forced to do things against the will of God and against their own will. What are the penalties for defiance they will have to endure for going against their oppressors? Some are abused and beaten, while others make the ultimate sacrifice, simply for expressing defiance.

Praying God's Word:

Oh God, all that You are is so overwhelming. I pray that my friends will always know that You are merciful. It really doesn't matter what we have done or where we are, You are perfect in Your execution of justice. Your justice is like no other. Your mercy is ever-ready and in full force to dismiss the penalties that have been piled up against us. Help us to appreciate Your mercy because sometimes we take it for granted. Help our friends who may not feel that they are deserving of Your mercy. They can feel or be led to believe that they are too far gone for mercy. Please Father, as deep as the ocean floor, let Your mercy drown every judgment against them.

Response:

_____

_____

_____

_____

_____

_____

DAY EIGHTEEN

The Backstory

Traffickers remove all choices from victims in order to maintain control. Situations are manipulated to benefit the trafficker's evil intentions.

"If you just behave, it will be easier. If you just do these things, it will get easier," my traffickers would tell me. It's a psychological game. You learn the system and what it takes to survive.

The traffickers impose their control. They break down your will and brainwash you to believe that you no longer have any choices except the ones they offer you. They give you a little freedom at a time: Little, micro choices. So first, by "cooperating," I got to choose how I wanted my tea or coffee. Then after a while I got to choose my own meal. Little by little I played the game, gaining the trust of the madam who was running the place, so that little by little I was able to get out to eat with some of the other girls. Girls who would then reinforce the system.

Amnesty International actually has a framework for understanding this dynamic, called Biderman's Chart of Coercion, which is used to explain the tactics used in controlling political prisoners or hostages.[22] It perfectly aligns with trafficker's behavior; the restriction of choices, for example, is called "monopolization of perception." Tactics designed to work on hostages, not surprisingly, work well on vulnerable girls and young women.

---

[22] Lloyd, p. 95.

Devotion Time

Please Read:

Jeremiah 29:11-13

Let's Pause and Consider:

"For I know the plans I have for you, declares the Lord, plans of welfare and not for evil, to give you a future and a hope" (v.11, ESV).

It is mind blowing for me to think that there is a God that already knows the plan for my life, and what paths I will take. Though I have sometimes struggled on the various paths chosen, I have found meaning within these struggles. The struggles have taught me important lessons and have helped build resilience and strength in me.

- What struggles have made you stronger?

Conversation:

We have so many ambitions and plans for our lives. We can sometimes become inundated by our plans and the plans others have for us. Sometimes, it seems like everyone has an opinion of what we should do, and how we should live our lives.

There are those who have completely lost the ability to choose. They no longer have a say in what they will eat or wear. They are not allowed to go too far from the reach of a human trafficker. They may be caged, locked up, rationed food and even denied sleep when exhaustion has taken over. These people have a different interpretation of the plans that others might have for them.

I don't know about you, but I am so very grateful that God's plans supersede and override any plans others may have for my life. His plans even overshadow the plans I sometimes make for myself. We serve a God who knows us better than we know ourselves. Many times we find certain paths difficult, not because we are not good at navigating the path, but because it is not good for us. I have learned, as I am sure many of you have, that it is always better to pray about how my plans work within the bigger picture. How my plans line up with the plans of God.

We know that He has plans for us. He knows what He wants for us. Even when we are not ready to accept His plans. His plans are timed with our preparedness.

Praying God's Word:

God, Your plans are perfect. Help us to submit to Your will. You know what is best for us. We allow You to freely take over our lives and to make us ready for Your plans. Even when the preparation seems more than what we are able to handle, be patient with us as we learn to trust You. Your plans for us are what we are searching for in our ambitions: Hope, peace, a bright future. God, we welcome Your plans into our hearts.

Response:

_____
_____
_____
_____
_____
_____

DAY NINETEEN

The Backstory

When a trafficking victim is ruthlessly tormented by abuse and manipulation, a life of peace is difficult to envision. Even upon rescue, survivors have been traumatized so badly that their brains no longer function in the proper way. The brain and body remain operating within a "fight, flight, or freeze" survival mode. Learning to heal from these psychological wounds is a long and sometimes painful process.

Since "Jane Doe" had barely seen the inside of a school since she was trafficked as a young teenage girl, one of our first priorities was to get her enrolled in high school. Still in survival mode, her fight-or-flight response was super-heightened after years of domination and control. So, when a group of boys started teasing her and pulling on her hair, "Jane" – unsurprisingly, given her history — responded with violence, beating the boys up. She got kicked out of school the same day she started.

Devotion Time

Please Read:

1 Timothy 2:1-4

Let's Pause and Consider:

"For kings and all who are in high positions, that we may lead a peaceable and quiet life, godly and dignified in every way" (v.2, ESV).

- What efforts do you make in your own life to create a sense of peace and tranquility?
- What is your plan of action to bring more peace into your daily living?

Conversation:

We live in a loud, disruptive and chaotic time and place. Regardless of your country or zip code, there seems to be a lack of peace. When I watch the news or listen to the radio, there seems to be a storm of problems and no place seems exempt. Is this what the world is coming to? A world dominated by such things as violence, hatred, and hostility?

I began to ask God for guidance on how to live in a society where everyone has their own agenda? This scripture spoke to my heart. It is simple, really. We are to live a quiet, peaceable life. We are to live in each tribe and nation in reverence to God. The prescription for our world's chaos is in Scripture.

I speak to many survivors of human trafficking who say, "This whole world is just messed up." These survivors have seen in their past more violence and abuse than most of us will ever be able to comprehend. For them, the world's current state is normal. So yes, they are correct. This world and our lives without Christ as the center, is messed up. However, there is a solution, a remedy. God has not left us alone in this regard. We have His desire, His heart so that we will be in constant fellowship with Him and at peace with our neighbors.

Praying God's Word:

God, I ask that You surround us with Your peace. A peace that the world can't ration nor extract from this earth. Let the peace that only comes from You fill our hearts and flood our nations. Only Your peace is powerful enough to be felt even in the most difficult of times. Please, grant us Your peace and let us be an example of that peace in our homes, in our jobs, and in our communities.

Response:

_____

_____

_____

_____

_____

_____

_____

DAY TWENTY

The Backstory

Survivors of human trafficking have had their trust broken time and time again. Traffickers gain the trust of their victims in order to manipulate them into submitting to their wills. Upon rescue, it is very difficult for survivors to learn who they can trust.

Devotion Time

Please Read:

Psalms 37:3-5

Let's Pause and Consider:

"Trust in the Lord, and do good; dwell in the land and befriend faithfulness" (v.3, ESV).

Sometimes the easiest way to learn whether we can trust a person is to simply give them our trust.

- When you have your trust in a person broken, how do you communicate your hurt? What is your style? Confrontational? Passive?
- How would your relationships with others benefit from personally working on your style?

Conversation:

There seems to be so much distrust. It is hard to know in whom we can confide, and who can be trusted. When I ask survivors to talk about the people they trust and with whom they can share their thoughts and feelings, they usually say that they have no one. These survivors, mostly women, do not have the utmost of confidence in any person. The people they trusted in the past turned their backs on them or broke that band of trust.

The traffickers are on the list of those not trustworthy since most victims were lied to as a way of gaining the victim's trust.

Unless we have been in the same situation as survivors, we will find it difficult at times to fully understand the scope of just how untrustworthy the world appears to them. Who can we share our secrets with in our most vulnerable moments? The circle of trust can be a very small one. The other part of trust is our emotions. Unless it is a professional therapist, we tend only to share these feelings and situations with those we care about.

As Christians, we know someone in whom we can trust and be confident that He will not use what He knows against us. He will not abandon us once we confess to Him. In fact, He wants us to share everything with Him. He wants us to put all our trust in Him. In fact, God offers a reward for trusting Him. If we continue reading verses four and five, we see that trusting God will cause us to have God's help and His blessings.

Praying God's Word:

I trust You. Into Your great hands I put my trust. I ask that You lead me to where my trust has no limits. God, I have been hurt by those I have trusted. Please allow me to rest in You and know that there is no better place for my trust than in Your arms.

Response:
_____
_____
_____
_____
_____
_____
_____

DAY TWENTY-ONE

The Backstory

When a victim is actively living in a state of survival, all efforts will be made to regain a sense of control in her life. Many survivors will gain legitimate employment and seek to "hoard" their money, or even hoard their food. She may keep these things close to her as if they are in short supply and in high demand. She is controlling her resources in case of a future shortage. This is a habit formed through years of a trafficker's abuses, as the trafficker may have withheld food, and any money a victim had earned would be controlled by the trafficker.

Devotion Time

Please Read:

Psalms 30:1-6

Let's Pause and Consider:

"For His anger is but for a moment, and His favor is for a lifetime. Weeping may tarry for the night, but joy comes in the morning" (v.5, ESV).

Personally speaking, it can be difficult for me to see joy when I'm facing a difficult situation. Over time, I have learned to slow down and ask myself:

- Is there anything about the situation that I can control?
- Is there anything that I can change?

In most cases, the answer is no. By learning to slow down and ask myself these questions before reacting, I drastically change my attitude towards the situation.

Conversation:

Joy is something that many of our trafficking survivors do not experience at the start. Yes, we all have moments of happiness no matter how small those moments may be. Joy ... Joy goes deeper than happiness. Happiness is based on our current situation, but joy goes beyond the moment. With joy, it doesn't matter what my external circumstance is because Joy is independent of what is going on in my life.

Our survivors do not have joy because most of them have experienced little that is good. Joy comes from knowing that God is in charge. It can be difficult to understand how one can have joy in the midst of difficult times. Joy is something that God gives to us when we understand there is nothing we are going through that He is not aware of.

Every problem that we face and encounter, God knows about it. When we understand this we know that stressing out isn't going to change anything. Having trust in God does bring about a change in our spirits. We can become joyful when we would otherwise be in tears. We have a childlike acceptance that God is going to take care of the problem, and therefore, we do not have to worry about it.

Praying God's Word:

Dear God, I am not upset by my current situation. It does not matter if things are going well or badly. I have a joy that goes beyond emotion. There is an inner peace that consoles me and lifts me up at the same time. God, I thank You for Your joy. Your joy is what I need to make it through each day. I can face every battle and obstacle because Your joy gives me strength to endure. I am so glad that Your joy causes each morning to dawn with new hope. Thank You for never taking Your joy away from me.

Response:

_____

_____

_____

_____

_____

_____

_____

DAY TWENTY-TWO

The Backstory

Most people know the difference between what is right and what is wrong. They know where they stand in terms of their personal values.

Once trafficked, victims are forced to perform acts that are completely against what they feel is right or wrong. It has been hammered into her that her only value lies in deeds that make her feel horrible about herself, and that what is right and wrong is determined by the whim of the trafficker. The victim loses her moral compass.

During the recovery process, survivors find a great deal of difficulty in moving beyond the actions they performed under force. They may even begin to identify themselves with the things they've done. Trafficking victims do not always see themselves as victims, often blaming themselves for their situation.[23]

Devotion Time

Please Read:

Jude 24

---

[23] Office for Victims of Crime, Training and Technical Assistance Center. *Human Trafficking Task Force e-Guide: Understanding Human Trafficking*. Retrieved from https://www.ovcttac.gov/taskforceguide/eguide/1-understanding-human-trafficking/

Let's Pause and Consider:

"Now to Him who is able to keep you from stumbling and to present you blameless before the presence of His glory with great joy" (v.24, ESV).

I feel that the majority of us can think of a few times in our lives when we have done things that we ultimately regret. It's difficult to think that these actions we've taken in the past can be forgiven, and that we have permission to move forward from these bad decisions.

- How tightly are you holding onto your past mistakes?
- How are these past mistakes impacting how you live now?

Conversation:

To be faultless of every sin that was committed against God ... It is amazing to me that a mighty God would consider me in His wonderful works. Unfortunately, I am not a perfect example. Don't get me wrong, we are made in the image and likeness of God, according to Genesis 1:26. Although we are wonderfully made, many times our lives, and at the very least, our behaviors, are not always wonderful.

God knows that we are a fallen creation. We have, over the course of generations, strayed further from God as we become more dependent on ourselves. The problem with getting further away from God is that we tend to become better acquainted with sin.

The young ladies who are in Rahab's Daughters' program usually say that they are to blame for their life's problems. They made the boyfriend (trafficker) upset, or they spoke with law enforcement when they should have kept their mouths closed. The scenarios of survivors viewing themselves as being at fault for one thing or another during their slavery is common. Much of this comes from being fed this belief that they are responsible by the person holding them by force.

It is a very tough life to constantly live in fear; to believe that if anything bad happens to you – whether or not it is within your control – it is your fault. You try to obey the trafficker's rules, even if they are to your detriment, because to break the rules results in violent punishment – and yet you can never escape being held responsible. The rules are unspoken, they constantly change, and often you don't know the rules until you break one, to dire consequences. You can only wait for the sentence when the accuser comes to rain judgment on you for breaking the rules.

I am so glad that God is not like man, especially the men and women who hold others captive. God is looking to justify us, to plead our case and to render us faultless of any and all wrongdoing. Not only does He make us faultless, but He gives us the tools we need to live a life that shows we are His redeemed. We were bought with the price of His life.

Praying God's Word:

Thank You for Your keeping power. You help me to stand firm when, on my own, my feet would stray from the righteous path. In the midst of my struggles, sometimes I do slip and fall, but You allow me to get up again, in Your grace. Because You have made me faultless, I can live a new life that is pleasing to You. Thank You for pleading my case and for never leaving my side. You are indeed both courtroom lawyer and righteous judge.

Response:

DAY TWENTY-THREE

The Backstory

Human trafficking victims are often starved, deprived of sleep, and deprived of other basic needs as a way for traffickers to maintain control. A sleep-deprived or starved person is often too fatigued to put up much resistance.

Prolonged sleep deprivation has been described as a "form of torture" because it waylays biological functions deep at the core of a person's mental and physical health. Sleep deprivation can cause, among other things: Feelings of fatigue, difficulties concentrating, and poor judgment—as well as a considerable increase in appetite. Coupled with the trafficker withholding food, the tactic's cruelty becomes magnified.[24]

In a 1940s University of Minnesota experiment, that could never be repeated today due to its cruelty and duress on human subjects, a group of men were starved for 24 weeks. Among their results, they found that: Prolonged semi-starvation produced significant increases in depression and hysteria; most participants experienced periods of severe emotional distress; many appeared apathetic and lethargic; and participants reported a decline in concentration, comprehension and judgment capabilities.[25]

---

[24] Bulkeley, K. (15 December 2014). Why Sleep Deprivation Is Torture. *Psychology Today*. Retrieved from https://www.psychologytoday.com/us/blog/dreaming-in-the-digital-age/201412/why-sleep-deprivation-is-torture

[25] Kaplan, B. and Rucklidge, J. (28 May 2013). Starvation: What Does it Do to the Brain? *Mad in America: Science, Psychiatry and Social Justice*. Retrieved from https://www.madinamerica.com/2013/05/starvation-what-does-it-do-to-the-brain/

Devotion Time

Please Read:

Isaiah 40:29-31

Let's Pause and Consider:

"He gives power to the faint, and to him who has no might He increases strength" (v.29, ESV).

Conversation:

We all want to be strong. To have exceptional strength so that we can defend ourselves and those we love. But sometimes our strength alone just isn't enough. There are those who would overpower us—and most human trafficking victims are overpowered every day. This is one of the reasons that they are not able to escape and run for freedom or even their lives. There are those who rule over them with a strong hand. To fight back feels like a losing battle, especially when they are already so weak and tired.

We sometimes overestimate our own strength. As we age, we learn that we may not have the same strength that we used to possess. This can be a very difficult realization to handle when we are being forced into a corner and are not strong enough to fight our way out.

God has provided us a way to escape. If we would just turn to Him and allow Him to lead us. He will give strength to the weak and He will strengthen the heart of the weary. Our human trafficking survivors are surviving because they have allowed God to fill their inner being with His strength. This strength enables them to continue moving forward when it seems they have reached a dead end. He increases their strength. And if they fall, He is going to pick them up again.

Praying God's Word:

God, I thank You for what You are doing in restoring the lives of survivors all over the world. Give them continued strength to know that this battle is not theirs, it is Yours. You have sustained them and enabled them to reach new heights. I ask that You continue to lift them higher, because they have put their assurance in You. Be their strong tower in time of trouble.

Response:

_____

_____

_____

_____

_____

_____

DAY TWENTY-FOUR

The Backstory

During the recovery process, many survivors want the transformation to be complete NOW, and to be healed immediately. Recovery is a process, and with any process, it takes time. Movement is taken step by step, at a consistent pace, so that the survivor is able to work towards building a sustainable future.

Devotion Time

Please Read:

James 1:2-4

Let's Pause and Consider:

"…for you know that the testing of your faith produces steadfastness…" (v.3, ESV).

Conversation:

I can honestly say that I need more patience. Most of us have limited patience when it comes to dealing with the long-term emotional needs of people outside of our inner circle. We are usually very concerned, just not very patient. Patience is something that we as believers say we have, and should have, but not every person does.

As we are living a life that represents Christ, there are situations and people who will come into our lives that test our patience. Even the best of us are tried with a situation or a person. However, that does not exempt us from being people of patience. Know that I write about myself, too, on this teaching. Think about our lives and how Christ has been exceedingly patient when dealing with us and our messes.

Victims of trafficking will come into our churches, schools, places of business, communities, and even into our lives. They are going to come with problems from their past and current situations. We are going to be challenged and tested to our utmost as they work through the dark memories and nightmares of their lives.

The Bible tells us that tests or trials help us build our patience. As our patience develops, scripture shares that we will lack nothing. God's word expresses to us that patience is the key to having a fulfilled life. My dealing with or acceptance of a victim and their emotional highs and lows not only shows the victim love, but also how my patience works in my favor.

Praying God's Word:

Father, thank You for Your patience towards us. We do not deserve it and we test it a lot. Help us to extend that patience that we experience from You to those around us and those outside of our circle. Bless our sisters and brothers, who need us to be patient with them, to receive us where we are, as our patience is nourished and developed.

Response:

DAY TWENTY-FIVE

The Backstory

Many survivors are held captive by shame long after they've been rescued from traffickers. This shame over what they did while under another person's control can be paralyzing and greatly hinder the recovery process, if not addressed. In more extreme cases, this shame may cause an individual to go back to a life of prostitution when he or she feels like they are not "good" for anything else.

Devotion Time

Please Read:

James 1:26-27

Let's Pause and Consider:

"If anyone thinks he is religious and does not bridle his tongue but deceives his heart, this person's religion is worthless" (v.26, ESV).

Conversation:

Our dear friends who have been trapped within the walls of modern-day slavery most times do not have much faith in God or the church. Many of them question the authenticity of those professing to be children of God as well as the God they profess to worship. As believers, we are watched even when we are not aware. As we do not always know who a trafficking victim might be, it's also difficult to know who's watching.

To say we are religious is like saying you are from the Royal British family. There is an expectation of what you will be like and how you will carry yourself. Unfortunately, a victim does not necessarily grasp that we are all sinners saved by grace. They sometimes forget that we are humans just like them and are flawed. When we say we are Christians, it is implied that we have a set of standards that we live by. We are religious, not because we practice rituals, but because we believe and follow the teachings of Christ.

Being a follower of Christ means that we are concerned about those who are less fortunate. It is our mission to share God's love and grace with those who have not had the best opportunities in life. When we use our resources to serve others, this touches the heart of God. If the truth is told, God doesn't care how big a church structure is. We are commissioned to build lives, not buildings. In other words, we are the church and our purpose and is not confined within the walls of a building. If our greatest accomplishment as believers is having a mega place of worship, but no love is shown for strangers or those in need, then we have missed one of our greatest opportunities as the church to show the heart of God. Let's not neglect to show concern for all people as we are all wonderfully made.

Praying God's Word:

Lord, help us understand that we must take initiative to live out Your teachings and worship beyond the walls of a building. Helps us to bring the Church to those who feel lost and alone. God, I ask that You keep our hearts focused on what is important to You. Help us to feel the pain of those who are suffering. We want to touch lives by expressing your heart and love for those who are so far away from you. Help us demonstrate compassion for those who are suffering and in need. Thank you for letting our light so shine that men, women, boys and girls will feel your heart through our lives.

Response:

DAY TWENTY-SIX

The Backstory

Many survivors seek fulfillment in their lives by using controlled substances or engaging in risky behavior. These behaviors also act to "numb" the inner pain that one may be experiencing.

Devotion Time

Please Read:

James 4:1-4

Let's Pause and Consider:

"You ask and do not receive, because you ask wrongly, to spend it on your passions" (v.3, ESV).

Conversation:

Worldliness is a spirit that has crept into the church. Although this topic is not popular, even though it is preached about, worldliness seems to be sitting on a pew in the local church, very relaxed. It is a spirit of deception and it only brings a wedge between our current situation and our divine destiny.

It is not possible to follow through with our purposeful mission having the same desires as the world. The world seeks self-gratifying pleasures, such as money, fame, attention, etc. As we are commissioned for greater purpose, we are to be neighbor-focused: What can we do to build others?

Those we serve during our community outreach are accustomed to the world and its lust and so-called pleasures. It is why they still yearn for more. The world's pleasures do not satisfy the desire to have fellowship with God, even if they aren't sure of what it is that's missing. We are to handle ourselves differently. We are to make an effort to live a life above reproach.

Scripture tells us that when we ask, and nothing happens, it's because our motives aren't right. When our motives are wrong we do not gain results. Children of God, I don't know about you, but I need my prayers answered. Whenever I, and our great teams are out ministering, we need God to show up. We never know what we will encounter and we need something to happen when we pray. Sometimes we even need a divine intervention on the spot.

It is important that we search our own hearts. We must uphold holiness. We cannot let the relaxed atmosphere of the world creep into the church. Lives are depending on us to be who we say we are, people of God, living in the world.

Praying God's Word:

Oh God, let us have a deeper desire to follow Your ways and to revere You. Our lives belong to You and not the world. We want to always put You first. We know that if we put You first, our prayers will be answered, and things will work out in our favor, if we would only seek Your kingdom.

Response:
_____
_____
_____
_____
_____
_____
_____

DAY TWENTY-SEVEN

The Backstory

There is a tendency for survivors to initially believe that their problems are too great to be healed. Unintentionally, they may use their problems as shields, a deterrent against those who may take advantage of them—as well as those who would truly help them. Throughout the recovery process, a survivor learns to humble herself and understand that she is capable of healing and has a right to receive the help to do so.

Devotion Time

Please Read:

2 Corinthians 10:1-4

Let's Pause and Consider:

"I, Paul, myself entreat you, by the meekness and gentleness of Christ — I who am humble when face to face with you, but bold toward you when I am away!"(v.1, ESV).

Conversation:

Meekness is a trait that seems rare. Meekness can be taken for weakness, but it is very much the opposite. One can be very strong and confident and still have a meek demeanor or spirit. Meekness is humility; to accept praise and not allow one's ego to rise up. When a believer walks humbly they do it intentionally, so that they will become less, in order for Christ to become greater.

When Paul is talking to the church at Corinth, he tells them that he is pleading in the meekness of Christ. But then he goes on to tell them how to do warfare, that we war in the spirit and not in the flesh. Paul is letting the church know that the only way to win the spiritual battles that you face and to intercede for others is to fight in meekness.

As I share above, meekness is not weakness. It is actually a sign of strength. When you know who you are in Christ, you can remain meek and humble. Our sisters and brothers who have been abused need us to know who we are in Christ. They do not need to hear loud prayers and beating of drums. What they do need is for us to operate in humility. Our warfare is won based on who we are in the kingdom. If we are to help our survivors break free from spiritual and emotional bondage, we must do it as Kingdom agents. We must do it as Paul, in the meekness and gentleness of Christ.

Praying God's Word:

God, I know it is difficult at times to break from the patterns that we have learned. I am asking that You give us the strength to know that meekness is actually greater in Your kingdom. We want to help our friends, who have suffered from the unthinkable abuse, to break free. We know that we may, on many occasions, have to intercede in prayer on their behalf. Keep our hearts pure and our spirits meek. We want to pull down stronghold, and we want victory to prevail in the lives of Your precious ones.

Response:

DAY TWENTY-EIGHT

The Backstory

Often, victims are stripped of their personal effects by their trafficker(s). These women, then, have nothing more than the clothing on their backs and even that may be too soiled for reuse. Upon rescue, these women are provided with new personal grooming items, clothing, food, and shelter.

Rahab's Daughters partners with organizations and individuals at all levels, from law enforcement to local safe houses, to meet survivors' every need.

Devotion Time

Please Read:

2 Corinthians 9:7-11

Let's Pause and Consider:

"Each one must give as he has decided in his heart, not reluctantly or under compulsion, for God loves a cheerful giver" (v.7, ESV).

Conversation:

I want to encourage you today. So many times, this scripture is quoted in relation to our financial giving to further the ministry of Christ. Today, I want you to know that giving also applies to your time and your talents.

Our time and the abilities God has given to us are precious and can be wasted if not used properly. We do not want to waste time doing anything that is not appreciated, and do not want to waste our talents on pointless things. My friends, I fully agree with you. I also know that when we work in ministry, in whatever area, there are times when we feel that the time that we are contributing is taken too lightly.

I, personally, have found in the past that I give and give and it sometimes seems as if my time is taken for granted. There have been occasions when I have worked with trafficking victims, that it seemed like I was just a chauffeur or personal organizer for what they needed and wanted. I really did not feel that what I was sacrificing, like time spent with friends or on personal care, was being appreciated.

I felt really badly about these feelings, because after all, these victims had gone through such horrible experiences and no one took what they wanted into consideration. I then began to read the Scriptures, and I came to 2 Corinthians 9. This opened my eyes and heart regarding the giving of my time in ways I had not considered before: no matter how much I give, I can never out-give God.

I want to encourage you not to lose heart. Your gift of your time and talents does not fall on uncultivated soil. It will take root. Not today and maybe not tomorrow, but the work you put into the lives of victims will produce tremendous reward. You know, we have heard in relation to giving financially, that we are giving "as unto the Lord." My friends, our giving of time and talents to those hurting also gives as unto the Lord.

When I put it in that perspective, I wanted to give more of my time, talents and finances. I did not simply want to be a benefactor of God's giving, I wanted to be a participant with Him in His giving.

Praying God's Word:

Father, I pray that You will strengthen our ability to give of our time and abilities, even when we do not feel appreciated. Our giving towards the building of Your kingdom, whether it is in time, resources or talents, are done to Your glory and not the praise and acceptance of men. Thank You for encouraging our hearts and keeping our focus on You.

Response:

_____

_____

_____

_____

_____

_____

_____

DAY TWENTY-NINE

The Backstory

Through relationship building and volunteerism, Rahab's Daughters can provide survivors with much needed resources. Each person we meet can uniquely fulfill a need required to help survivors rebuild a healthy lifestyle.

Devotion Time

Please Read:

1 Corinthians 12:12-13

Let's Pause and Consider:

"For just as the body is one and has many members, and all the members of the body, through many, are one body, so it is with Christ" (v.12, ESV).

Conversation:

Every believer no matter who they are or where they have come from, whether rich or poor, no matter their religious affiliation, is a member of Christ's body, with definite gifts. Now, whether or not we tap into that gift is a different story and will have to be part of my next book. Know that your gift is vital to God's work.

We all have a path in life. Our paths lead us to different places and different people. How we choose to use, or not use, the gift we have been given is completely up to us. Know that in the absence of our gift, a life may never be changed.

Now, I know you can have more than one ministry gift. For the sake of this devotional we will group all of your gifts into one. Your ability to do what no one else can do exactly like you is paramount to winning hearts to Christ. I have heard people say that they don't have any gifts for ministry or that what they bring to the table is insignificant. Paul tells the church at Corinth that all are members of the body of Christ, and therefore, all have been given a gift for the building of the Kingdom of God.

When I meet victims of trafficking for the first time, one of the things that usually pops into my mind is: what is your ministry gift? I know there is one inside of this person, just waiting to be cultivated and used for great work. When we fail to operate our gifts, we fail to allow the spirit of God to work through us. Healings, knowledge, wisdom, or whichever gift you have been given, should not be kept inside and never utilized. Ignoring your gift robs the Spirit of His own resources with which you were entrusted.

Do not be afraid or shy to use your gift. You are special in the kingdom of God and so is your gift. It doesn't matter how many people pray, no one can pray like you. It doesn't matter how many people are wise, no one has your wisdom. You are instrumental to helping human trafficking survivors break free from bondage and emotional instability. You are the key to their hearts being softened and opened to hearing the good news of Jesus the Christ. You are the key! Without you, change won't happen. I know that's a lot of pressure, I get it. But the joy will flood your soul when you operate your gift.

Praying God's Word:

Let the words of our mouths and the meditation of our hearts be acceptable. God, help me to use what You freely gave to me. I want to be instrumental in the building of Your kingdom. I know that my gift is unique and is needed. Bless me to overcome my fears or hesitations and allow me to trust that You, who gave me this gift, will use it for Your glory.

Response:

_____

_____

_____

_____

_____

_____

DAY THIRTY

The Backstory

"Survival sex" is a term that the general population doesn't often hear. It is a form of trafficking. Survival sex is when a person prostitutes him/herself in exchange for basic necessities such as housing or food. This person will use prostitution because he or she feels that their body is all that they have left that is of value.

Devotion Time

Please Read:

Luke 18:1-8

Let's Pause and Consider:

"And he told them a parable to the effect that they ought always to pray and not lose heart" (v. 1, ESV).

Conversation:

When we pray for ourselves or others, it can seem as if nothing is happening to change the situation. Victims of human trafficking have shared stories of how they prayed and prayed for someone to find them and rescue them. How they just kept praying and sometimes, even when they were forced to do something, they would focus not on what was happening at that moment, but instead pray that someone would come in to help them.

When trafficking victims are rescued, they tend to do two things first: eat and say "thank you Jesus," or some version of gratitude for divine intervention. They are hungry from not being fed, and they know that their prayers were answered. They did not lose heart even though it did not get any easier for them. They trusted and believed that God heard them, because they had no other deliverer. Wow …!

Haven't you done this? When you are overwhelmed with a problem that you know you cannot change on your own, you pray. I do it, too. In Luke, we see that Christ tells the people that prayer should be a consistent action in their lives. They are to pray and hold on to the promises of God, pray and not lose heart.

When we pray for survivors, we pray believing that Heaven will respond. Luke 18 tells the parable of the judge who tends to the woman's request because she would not leave him alone. God is a just and righteous judge who gave His son for us, how much more will He tend to our cry if we call Him?

Praying God's Word:

God, we want to always be in communication with You. We do not just want to call You in times of trouble, but we want to pray as You showed us, continually. Thank You for answering the prayers of so many survivors. We know that You are a prayer-answering God. We await more praise reports of how You became someone's knight in shining armor. Thank You so much for giving ear to our requests and for granting us the right to call You in times of trouble.

Response:

DAY THIRTY-ONE

The Backstory

So many trafficking survivors come from homes that may have been plagued with abuse prior to the individual becoming trafficked. As a University of Massachusetts study found, looking at young people who had been trafficked or were at high risk to be, "A common theme was experience with family violence including physical, sexual and emotional abuse; abuse of siblings by parents or parent-figures; attempts they made to protect siblings from abuse; violence they perpetrated themselves or were accused of perpetrating, and witnessing violence between adults."[26]

In recovery, a survivor not only has to address the trauma experienced while being trafficked, but she may also have to address the things that led to her becoming so vulnerable in the first place. These abuses more than likely occurred at a very young age, and trying to understand the "why", is often a lost cause and has little to do with the young girl.

The most important healing that can take place is through unconditional, non- judgmental love. This type of love contributes to the building up of the survivor through faith.

---

[26] Williams, L.M. & Frederick, M.E., p. 22.

Devotion Time

Please Read:

Titus 3: 1-7

Let's Pause and Consider:

"To speak evil of no one, to avoid quarreling, to be gentle, and to show perfect courtesy toward all people. For we ourselves were once foolish, disobedient, led astray, slaves to various passions and pleasures, passing our days in malice and envy, hated by others and hating one another" (v. 2-3, ESV).

Conversation:

We are to build each other up on our most holy faith. We are hit every day with some new stressor that needs attention, whether from work, family, etc. It can begin to burden the best of us. All we need is for someone to encourage us and to be in a corner cheering for us.

Titus admonishes us to lift each other and to not to let our proud Christian walk cause us not to behave in a Godly manner. We can sometimes look down on people based upon their current situation in life or from what they have been delivered. We should not be Christian snobs. In Titus, we are shown what Godly exhortation should be.

Survivors of human trafficking have told me how they are hesitant to go inside of a church or a religious setting. They feel that "church folk" can be the most judgmental. Survivors have shared that they get looks because they don't dress like other people or talk like them. They tend to sit in the back because they know they will be exiting this place very soon.

We should NEVER have a house of worship where people, no matter who they are or where they come from, do not feel the love of Christ. Titus reminds us that our own lives were once messed up. In verse three, Titus names a few of the evils from which most of us were delivered. I am certain that at least one of these evils covers the past of every born-again believer.

This isn't to bring up sins or errors of the past, but to ask that we remember to love and to lift up each person with whom we come in contact. We should not judge someone based on hairstyle, dress, or cleanliness. These things mean absolutely nothing and should not stand in the way of us sincerely being the first to say "welcome." When I speak about human trafficking to church congregations, I always share that "we do not know what that person had to escape in order to walk through these church doors." Let us make sure that our welcome is a positive and lasting impression, one that is not based on any form of judgment.

Praying God's Word:

God, thank You for using me to lift up others. I want to encourage someone who is burdened. It doesn't matter who it is or what they look like. God, You came to me when I did not look, smell, or act in the way I do now. Help me to exalt and build others so that Your love and Your mercy will be felt.

Response:

_____

_____

_____

_____

_____

_____

NOTES

BIBLIOGRAPHY

Bulkeley, K. (15 December 2014). Why Sleep Deprivation Is Torture. Psychology Today. Retrieved from https://www.psychologytoday.com/us/blog/dreaming-in-the-digital-age/201412/why-sleep-deprivation-is-torture

Coffey, John. (2007). The abolition of the slave trade: Christian conscience and political action. Retrieved from http://www.jubilee-centre.org/the-abolition-of-the-slave-trade-christian-conscience-and-political-action-by-john-coffey/

Friedman, S. (2005). Who is there to help us: How the system fails sexually exploited girls in the United States. New York: EPCAT-USA, Inc.

Gates, Jr., H. L. How many slaves landed in the U.S.? The African Americans: Many Rivers to Cross. PBS.org. Retrieved from https://www.pbs.org/wnet/african-americans-many-rivers-to-cross/history/how-many-slaves-landed-in-the-us/

Geiger, E. & Peck, K. (2016). Designed to Lead. Nashville, TN: B&H Publishing Group

Har, Janie. (March 2, 2013). Is the average age of entry into sex trafficking between 12 and 14 years old? Politifact.com. Retrieved from https://www.politifact.com/oregon/statements/2013/mar/02/diane-mckeel/Is-average-age-entry-sex-trafficking-between-12-an/

Hounmenou, Charles. (2015). Human Trafficking in Illinois Fact Sheet. Jane Addams Center for Social Policy and Research, Jane Addams College of Social Work. Chicago, IL: University of Illinois at Chicago. Retrieved from https://socialwork.uic.edu/wp-content/uploads/bsk-pdf-manager/FINAL_-_Human_TraffickinginIllinoisFactSheet-November2015_2_121.pdf

Human Rights First. (September 2017). Human Trafficking by the Numbers. Retrieved from https://www.humanrightsfirst.org/resource/human-trafficking-numbers

Hybels, B. (1995). *Rediscovering Church: The Story and Vision of Willow Creek Community Church.* Michigan: Zondervan Publishing House

Institute of Medicine and National Research Council. (2013). Confronting Commercial Sexual Exploitation and Sex Trafficking of Minors in the United States. Washington, DC: The National Academies Press. Retrieved from https://www.nap.edu/read/18358/chapter/6

International Labor Organization (2005). A global alliance against forced labour. Global report under the follow-up to the ILO Declaration on Fundamental Principles and Rights at Work, ILO 93rd Session 2005

Kaplan, B. and Rucklidge, J. (28 May 2013). Starvation: What Does it Do to the Brain? Mad in America: Science, Psychiatry and Social Justice. Retrieved from https://www.madinamerica.com/2013/05/starvation-what-does-it-do-to-the-brain/

Lloyd, Rachel. (2011). *Girls Like Us: Fighting for a World Where Girls are Not for Sale.* New York: HarperCollins Publishers

Mabilog, Patrick. (23 November 2016). 3 Reasons Why the Church is the Hope of the World. Christian Today. Retrieved from https://www.christiantoday.com/article/3-reasons-why-the-church-is-the-hope-of-the-world/101606.htm

National Institute of Justice. (2019). Human Trafficking. Retrieved from https://www.nij.gov/topics/crime/human-trafficking/pages/welcome.aspx

National Runaway Safeline. (2019). Retrieved from https://www.1800runaway.org/2008/07/getting-home-free/

Office for Victims of Crime, Training and Technical Assistance Center. Human Trafficking Task Force e-Guide: Understanding Human Trafficking. Retrieved from https://www.ovcttac.gov/taskforceguide/eguide/1-understanding-human-trafficking/

Polaris Project. (January 5, 2016). The Average Age of Entry Myth. Retrieved from: https://polarisproject.org/blog/2016/01/05/average-age-entry-myth

UN News. (29 July 2016). "Only one out of 100 people are rescued" from human trafficking. Retrieved from https://news.un.org/en/audio/2016/07/615462

Williams, L.M. & Frederick, M.E. (2009). *Pathways into and out of commercial sexual victimization of children: Understanding and responding to sexually exploited teens.* Lowell, MA: University of Massachusetts Lowell.

Wolffe, John; Harrison, B. (May 2006) [online edition; first published September 2004], "Wilberforce, William (1759–1833)", Oxford Dictionary of National Biography, Oxford University Press. Retrieved from http://www.oxforddnb.com/view/10.1093/ref:odnb/9780198614128.001.0001/odnb-9780198614128-e-29386;jsessionid=49747F9F4B67B476FF661E23682C08DE

PGIL2024USA